Counselling for
Asperger Couples

of related interest

**Marriage and Lasting Relationships with Asperger's
Syndrome (Autism Spectrum Disorder)**
Successful Strategies for Couples or Counselors
Eva A. Mendes
Foreword by Stephen M. Shore
ISBN: 978-1-84905-999-2
eISBN: 978-0-85700-981-4

Asperger Syndrome (Autism Spectrum Disorder) and Long-Term Relationships
Second Edition
Ashley Stanford
Foreword by Liane Holliday Willey
ISBN: 978-1-84905-773-8
eISBN: 978-1-78450-036-8

Troubleshooting Relationships on the Autism Spectrum
A User's Guide to Resolving Relationship Problems
Ashley Stanford
ISBN: 978-1-84905-951-0
eISBN: 978-0-85700-808-4

The Other Half of Asperger Syndrome (Autism Spectrum Disorder)
A Guide to Living in an Intimate Relationship with a Partner who is on the Autism Spectrum
Second Edition
Maxine Aston
Foreword by Tony Attwood
ISBN: 978-1-84905-498-0
eISBN: 978-0-85700-920-3

The Asperger Couple's Workbook
Practical Advice and Activities for Couples and Counsellors
Maxine Aston
ISBN: 978-1-84310-253-3
eISBN: 978-1-84642-851-7

22 Things a Woman with Asperger's Syndrome Wants Her Partner to Know
Rudy Simone
Illustrated by Emma Rios
Foreword by Tony Attwood
ISBN: 978-1-84905-883-4
eISBN: 978-0-85700-586-1

22 Things a Woman Must Know If She Loves a Man with Asperger's Syndrome
Rudy Simone
Illustrated by Emma Rios
Foreword by Maxine Aston
ISBN: 978-1-84905-803-2
eISBN: 978-1-84642-945-3

When Herscue Met Jomphrey and Other Tales from an Aspie Marriage
Herscue Bergenstreiml
ISBN: 978-1-84905-696-0
eISBN: 978-1-78450-211-9

Counselling for
Asperger Couples

Barrie Thompson
Foreword by Steve Bagnall

Jessica Kingsley *Publishers*
London and Philadelphia

First published in 2008
by Jessica Kingsley Publishers
73 Collier Street
London N1 9BE, UK
and
400 Market Street, Suite 400
Philadelphia, PA 19106, USA

www.jkp.com

Printed digitally since 2016

Library of Congress Cataloging in Publication Data
A CIP catalog record for this book is available from the Library of Congress

British Library Cataloguing in Publication Data
A CIP catalogue record for this book is available from the British Library

ISBN 978 1 84310 544 2
eISBN 978 1 84642 831 9

Dedicated to my brother Derek

Acknowledgements

I should like to thank all of those clients who were bold enough to step into the world of Asperger counselling. I will be eternally grateful to them. In many ways they have enabled me to make more sense of my own life. They know who they are and I can only hope that I have given back to them in equal measure.

I have a very high regard for Relate as a counselling service. I want to thank the national office for providing me with a platform from which I could go on to do my research work into Asperger Syndrome, but I want to particularly thank my supervisor, management team and colleagues at Relate Coventry for their support in the work I undertake.

Most of all I want to thank my wife Dilys for her unending support, without which my counselling work and this book would not have been possible.

Contents

FOREWORD 9

INTRODUCTION 13

Chapter 1 Stage One: Understanding Asperger Syndrome 17

Chapter 2 Stage Two: Individual Counselling 22

Chapter 3 Stage Three: Co-Counselling Begins 31

Chapter 4 Stage Four: Acknowledging Different
Perspectives 41

Chapter 5 Stage Five: Visual Aids for Understanding:
What the Counsellor Does 56

Chapter 6 Stage Six: Developing Strategies:
What the Clients Do 88

Chapter 7 Stage Seven: Ongoing Support and
Personal Space 122

Chapter 8 Conclusion – Where Are We Now? 134

REFERENCES 139

INDEX 141

Foreword

Some years ago, when I was working as Deputy Chief Executive of Relate, I received a letter urging us to do more for couples where one partner had Asperger Syndrome (AS). In fact the letter was quite critical of us, so I wanted to respond positively. But it was very difficult to respond positively as most of our workforce had probably never heard of AS. There was little prospect of introducing it as a topic in our already crammed basic training programmes, and there was little demand. People were not coming to us specifically asking for help in making successful relationships where one partner had been diagnosed with AS.

But the letter clearly had a point. If one partner had AS this was potentially a huge issue for the couple unless they could find successful strategies. At the same time many couples were struggling with this without even knowing it. They had not heard of AS, or, even if they had, no diagnosis had been given or thought of. We put on a one-day course for our counsellors, but it was merely scratching the surface. All we were able to do was to raise awareness of AS as a potential issue for some of the many thousands of couples and individuals we saw each year.

And that was that. There was no question of developing a model of how we could work more effectively with couples where one partner had AS. We didn't have the capacity, there still wasn't the demand and we didn't have anyone to do it; anyone to champion the issue. Then one day Barrie Thompson walked into my office and asked me to supervise his Masters degree dissertation on working with couples where one partner had AS. Naturally, I tried to put him off. Good topic, but he needed not only to be able to find enough couples, but they needed to be willing and able to talk with him, to be a part of his research. He'd never do it. It was impracticable!

Needless to say, he did do it, notwithstanding his full-time 'day job'. He had already thought a lot about it and had tracked down the relatively few other people with the same interest, like Maxine Aston and Digby Tantam. He used his contacts and the Relate network to find couples he could talk with and we spent a fascinating year meeting to talk and think through the issues that were emerging. Did you need to know you had AS, or have a diagnosis, or was it just that you needed to recognise that certain patterns and behaviours might be an obstacle in your relationship? Were we all AS anyway, somewhere along a very wide spectrum? Does a label make things better or worse? He hadn't developed a model for working with couples at that stage, but it was the beginning and he clearly was not going to leave it at that once the dissertation was written.

That was more than five years ago and this book shows just how far things have moved on. People have heard of AS. Maybe they have read an article in a popular magazine. Maybe they are aware of children receiving extra help at school with AS related difficulties, and realised too that these children grow up and form their own couple relationships. So people nowadays are more likely to recognise AS and more likely to ask for help. This book shows there is help. Barrie does not overplay this. There is no cure on offer in this text, no false hope, but the real hope that comes from a systematic model with a host of ideas and techniques forged in discussion with real couples. There is honesty and realism and that is its power. When you can say with authority, 'I have talked to scores of couples in this situation and this is what they say they have found helpful,' people will hang on your every word. But neither is this a blueprint. It's a model for helping, not a formula that works by rote. Each couple is unique and though you might use some of the specific strategies in this book, the book is more than that. It gives a strategy for forming strategies and devising helping tasks bespoke to each couple, each situation. That is the art and skill of it, and like all the best ideas its power is in its simplicity.

Why then does this matter? It matters because couple relationships are a fundamental building block of our society. It matters because the building blocks won't hold together without understanding and inclusion of all types of people, including those with AS and their partners. So this raises wider social policy issues too, ones that politicians are not very good at dealing with. Politicians continue to squirm away from 'couples' as a social policy issue for fear of recommending one family structure and condemning others, or embrace the issue and then make a total hash of their response akin to a moth's relationship to the flame. The political catchphrase 'back to basics' has haunted politicians of all parties for more than ten years. Nevertheless, I sense this will be an issue again at the next election. There is already argument about the so-called 'couple penalty' in the tax and benefit system. But just funding services for couples might be a better, quicker and cheaper start. I never met a couple yet who got a calculator out to measure their net tax and benefit gain/loss if they got together or split up and then used that as a key factor in their decision. But I have met a lot of couples and individuals who could not get basic relationship counselling when they needed it because they could not afford it! This is a book about practice not politics, but the practice described here needs to be accessible to the couples that need it. It needs to be on offer and that is a political issue.

This book also matters because 'evidence-based practice' matters. If private or public money goes into developing and maintaining services for couples, people want to know 'Does it work?' What was the outcome?' This book gives an answer to those key questions through its clear case studies.

Overall this book says, not just that couples matter, but that AS couples matter. That you don't have to believe, or follow, the counsel of gloom offered by a minority of friends and relatives you will meet in this book. There is hope. This is true not just for the couples living with AS who have had the courage to recognise the issue and do something about it, it's potentially true for anyone in any family relationship. There is no panacea, no guarantee, but there is always the hope of finding the small, often very simple step that makes a big difference.

Steve Bagnall
former Deputy Chief Executive of Relate

Introduction

Born and brought up in Caterham, Surrey in the 1950s, I had no reason to suspect that my childhood was any different to that of my four older siblings or, indeed, of my peers at school. A brief reflection of those days suggests they were happy ones, but deeper recollections evoke memories of more problematic times and suggest that the happy days were only so if they were on my terms! With personal problems born out of obsessive-compulsive behaviour, rituals, obsessional interests, physical tics and temper meltdowns. I was, according to my brothers and sisters, a difficult child. What brought about these behaviours is a tricky question for me to answer, but certainly they existed and created numerous difficulties for me, including isolation from all but a very few of my peers.

I'm not sure how aware my father was of my behaviour and mannerisms, as he seemed to be at work a lot, usually coming home after I had gone to bed. I believe my mother took the view that I would just 'grow out of it' and, although very loving, she never seemed to make an issue of my issues.

My principal obsession was football, but as a child it was not participating in the team sport that obsessed me, it was reading anything and everything remotely connected with football; relentlessly drawing football related pictures and spending endless hours on my own, just me, juggling a football. The irony of this particular obsession is that in my teenage years my two-footed ability with a football had the effect of creating for me a network of 'friends' in the various teams that I was asked to play for. I think my team mates had mixed feelings about me in that I never used to pass the ball or say much to them, but I scored plenty of solo goals and the teams I played for enjoyed much success. In any event, because of my football skills I was accepted and over the course of many years I became more of a team player, both on and off the field.

I have always thought in pictures and I see Asperger Syndrome (AS) problems in much the same way. I see the person with AS standing on one side of a river with questions, but no answers; problems, but no solutions. The answers and solutions lie on the other side, but as yet they can't be seen or reached and the river holds many dangers from the speed at which it flows, its undercurrents and some potentially threatening occupants. How to get to the other side, to find answers and solutions, is the purpose of this book.

It was whilst working as a couple counsellor for Relate that I first heard the term 'Asperger Syndrome' and was immediately able to identify with it. My interest in the subject grew and, as a consequence of studying the disorder whilst undertaking my Masters degree, I now feel able to offer a solution in the form of a counselling model to aid people to cross that river; to have the opportunity of discovering the answers and solutions they have been seeking, or indeed to realise, perhaps for the first time, that within their relationship with their spouse or partner exists a problem that hitherto had been unknown to them.

The first seven chapters of this book represent the seven stages of the model in the order they are applied in the counselling process. The model allows for the stages to be revisited if and when appropriate. It will be seen by the reader as they progress through the book that a previous stage can be revisited if necessary, for example, if further exploration and understanding of an AS issue (Stage Four) has to be undertaken after some initial strategies or tasks (Stage Six) have been carried out by the client couple.

Chapter 1 briefly describes how I came to know about AS, but more importantly for the reader explains where and how knowledge of AS can be gained for their own benefit, this being a fundamental part of Stage One of my counselling model. Chapter 2 explains that initial counselling should be separate for both partners so that their own needs can be addressed before co-counselling starts. Chapter 3 is where the partners begin counselling together and embark on the process of developing a conjoint understanding of AS issues and personality differences. Chapter 4 develops communication between the couple and generates a better understanding of each partner's perspectives. Chapter 5 makes use of genograms, lists, flip chart diagrams and any other form of drawing, usually done by the counsellor to aid understanding between the couple. Chapter 6 takes this one stage further by allowing the clients (where possible) to develop their own lists, strategies and tasks. Chapter 7 encourages the partners of people with AS to have their own space and time, and where possible to join (or even form) support groups. Support, both internal and external to the couple relationship is discussed here for the person with AS also. Finally, Chapter 8 gives a conclusion that includes a view of where we are now in terms of counselling opportunities for Asperger couples, now that a model is available to assist them in creating a better relationship for themselves.

It seems apparent that there are different levels of understanding of AS required according to the role and the needs of the individual. Whilst this book is primarily about couples where one partner has AS, the strategies and tactics described here to generate understanding, improve communication and generally enrich the quality of life of those who are touched by AS, can be used by counsellors, therapists, parents and teachers as well as couples affected by AS who, for whatever reason are not in counselling at that time or, as is more likely to be the case, have no access to a counsellor or therapist trained in AS issues.

With regard to parents using the strategies in this book for their children, most of the strategies can be used effectively with older children and adolescents. For younger children some of them will be suitable, others may seem too advanced, but with some imagination may be adapted, whilst some may be entirely inappropriate. In each case the parents will know their child well enough to be able to determine if a particular strategy is appropriate for them or not, or they may seek the advice of their child's teacher to see if they feel a particular strategy is suitable. It should be remembered that age is not the only criterion that should be considered when using these strategies. There are probably many bright young children who would put these strategies to as good a use as their older counterparts.

I hope that my experiences, my research and my model will have meaning for couples where AS or its traits are a presenting problem. I stress the importance of 'traits' because I don't consider a formal diagnosis of AS to be necessary (unless the client does). What is important is the recognition by the couple that AS or its traits is negatively affecting their relationship and that they are willing to try to make positive changes.

Quoting Christopher Slater-Walker from *An Asperger Marriage*:

> It is quite clear that there is little or no help available in the United Kingdom for couples or even individuals in our situation. Some kind of regular professional counselling, however uncomfortable it may be at first, where we could be brought together in a neutral situation, and each given individual advice on avoiding past situations and to work towards future improvements, would be enormously valuable. (Slater-Walker and Slater-Walker 2002, p.157)

I believe that my model goes a long way in addressing the shortfalls in specialist counselling that Christopher describes, but I feel it goes further than offering just *individual* advice, it also offers advice, guidance and support to the couple. I also believe that counsellors, therapists and other professionals will be able to identify with its simple methodology for offering help to such couples.

Pseudonyms have been used to represent the clients that I write about in this book, but where a particular quote from a client may identify them (if only to themselves), their permission has been sought for it to be used.

In keeping with other books and papers about this subject, Asperger Syndrome will be regularly abbreviated to AS and non-AS or neurotypical people will be regularly referred to as NTs.

Chapter 1

Stage One: Understanding Asperger Syndrome

Knowledge is of two kinds. We know a subject ourselves, or we know where we can find information on it.

Samuel Johnson

Asperger Syndrome is defined by what is termed the 'Triad of Impairment'. This triad relates to communication, socialisation and imaginative thinking.

Communication suffers in the person with AS due to the inappropriate use of speech, facial expression, voice intonation, gestures and other non-verbal language as well as delayed language processing and limited or non-existent eye contact.

Poor socialisation is exemplified by difficulties in either forming or maintaining relationships, a lack of empathy, poor social timing and skills and either part or total body-contact rejection.

Imaginative thinking, or the lack of, is typified by obsessional or ritualistic behaviour, an emphasis on egocentric thoughts and rigid or inflexible thinking where the views of others are difficult for the person with AS to understand. It is important to stress that the elements of the triad are in themselves a spectrum in which people with AS can be affected differently.

Other aspects or traits of the condition can include a tendency to apply a literal meaning to words and therefore being unable to comprehend innuendos, analogies or the like; a strong sense of order within their lives where a rule-bound and regulated life such as being in certain occupations gives the person the boundaries they need; a strong sense of order and sameness; being clumsy and having poor motor skills and spatial awareness; having a narrow and sometimes intense range of interests, and sensory overload where excesses of noise, colour, smell or movement may cause anxiety and prove to be distressing. Again, it is important to stress that all of these traits may not occur in the same person, but if they do they may well vary in their intensity.

In his quote at the start of this chapter Samuel Johnson makes a distinction between knowing a subject personally and impersonally. But is knowing a subject the same as understanding it? In certain situations it can be, but one can read a book about the First World War and have a comprehensive knowledge of it, but not possess the understanding had by those who were knee-deep in mud, surrounded by the corpses of those who were once their friends, whilst feeling cold, hungry and scared, as bullets and bombs rained about them day after day, month after month.

Or one can watch a Grand Prix race on television and be excited by the action, but not understand the thrill and exhilaration of driving such a powerful motor car around a hairpin bend at 90 mph or along the grandstand straight in excess of 200 mph.

So with AS, is the difference between knowing about it and understanding it the same as objectively observing it and subjectively experiencing it? Of course, other people can experience its effects from a different perspective, namely the spouses, partners, parents and children of people with AS, but this is a different perception; one that looks in on AS from the outside and has a different understanding of it than the person who experiences it at first hand. Indeed, during one session one of my clients said, 'My wife sees me compensate with my AS when I'm with other people and she thinks I should compensate more with her. What she doesn't realise is that I put on an act with other people; I don't want to put on an act with my wife.' He went on to say, 'Knowledge about AS is one thing and I'm glad my wife possesses the knowledge that she does, but it's not the same as being personally handicapped by it on a day-by-day basis. When people see me acting "normally", nothing actually changes in my head – I just have to try to do things as people would expect me to and it's not easy. They just don't realise just how hard I have to work to do that.'

I've had numerous clients where the neuro-typical (NT) partner has had an impressive knowledge of the subject, but (understandably) little awareness of how the condition has the potential to both strain and constrain those who have it. I have also had AS clients who lacked either knowledge or understanding of their own condition, as they assumed that their view on the world was exactly the same as everyone else's. The skill, I believe, is to try to balance knowledge with understanding and to try to use this dual approach to attempt to discover the perspective of the 'other' person, irrespective of whether they are the AS or NT person in the relationship.

For my own part, I came to understand AS in both of the ways Samuel Johnson describes; by knowing it from a personal perspective (which can be illuminating, but is nonetheless a very subjective experience), and by finding out as much information as I could on the subject in the course of my academic research. My research included reading numerous books and academic papers as well as conducting interviews with couples who had already undergone couple counselling because one of the partners had AS, and the impact of the AS on the relationship had been a negative one. It goes without saying that if AS had a positive impact upon a relationship (a very unlikely scenario) then counselling wouldn't have been necessary.

I had hoped to get a client-centred perspective on what interventions learned from counselling most affected their relationships, and what they thought would be important interventions to include in counselling AS couples. I certainly wasn't disappointed, as most of the interviewees expressed views about the counselling they underwent as having some positive impact upon them, but that there needed to be more research and insight into AS. Whilst there had been some useful interventions (see below), some interviewees went on to say that their positive expectations at the point of entry into couple counselling had not been fully realised because of a lack of knowledge and understanding of AS, and not only did their relationship not improve, it was actually put under more strain than was previously the case. One interviewee told me, 'We struggled for a long time to find a counsellor who knew about Asperger Syndrome and when we eventually thought we had, it turned out he didn't understand our situation at all. Instead of making things better between us, things became more difficult.'

However, a positive outcome of those interviews is that I believe I was privileged to undergo *real* learning from *real* people in *real* situations. Indeed so valuable to me were some of the comments, I feel I should share them with you so that you may benefit from them also. Whilst the quotes of the interviewees are real, for reasons of confidentiality the names applied to them are not.

> Increased awareness allows me to see certain situations that I can then talk about; it also increases mutual respect. (John, a husband with AS)

> The counsellor having knowledge of AS makes them able to differentiate between issues that are most likely to be a product of the AS, and other problems that may not be. (Ann, whose husband has AS)

> My wife would have benefited from more individual counselling perhaps. She needed more assurance, more support perhaps. (Peter, a husband with AS)

> A number of sessions on my own with the counsellor would have been very useful before co-counselling began. Then I could have discussed my feelings, my needs and how these might be met. (Jane, whose husband has AS)

Having things written down, e.g. diagrams, flip-charts, hand-outs, helps me when I'm trying to understand things. (Michael, a husband with AS)

The genogram was very helpful. It particularly helped Michael as he understands things better when they are written down. We can then take these things home and look at them together. This applies to things that are written or drawn. (Louise, wife of Michael, above)

We use lists to aid memory and to develop conjoint and agreed routines. (Dawn, whose husband has AS)

A support group for my wife would be very helpful. (Alan, a husband with AS)

Doing things apart from my husband – me having women friends is very important. (Rachel, whose husband has AS)

AS people need to be asked if they understand what's being said to them, don't assume they do. Ask them for their perceptions and views – people with AS need clear and unambiguous messages or instructions. (Sue, whose husband has AS)

By audio-recording all of the interviews during my research, I was then able to have these transcribed into a typed format. A subsequent analysis of these transcripts enabled me to classify all of my interviewees' comments into seven various themes. It is these themes that came to form the stages of my counselling model. Each stage is here represented as a separate chapter of this book.

How much of an understanding of AS a person needs will usually depend upon the purpose to which they wish to apply that understanding. For example, psychologists, therapists and couple counsellors wishing to work in this particular field would probably need to know and understand more than a GP; the latter presumably requiring only sufficient knowledge of the subject in order to refer clients to the former.

Special Needs teachers working with children with AS would need a more comprehensive understanding of autism and AS than solicitors, for example, who may have absolutely no knowledge whatsoever, but may have to obtain a rudimentary understanding for the initial legal processes to take place (e.g. representing a suspect with AS in an interview at a police station or an initial appearance at court). If, however, the matter should go to trial before a judge and jury, the solicitor or barrister may need to employ the services of an expert witness; someone who has a high degree of knowledge and understanding of the subject.

How, then, can we promote knowledge and understanding about AS? Staying with Samuel Johnson's quote from the beginning of this chapter, I am first of all going to recommend certain books that I believe relate to certain general age groups.

My Social Stories Book, by Carol Gray and Abbie Leigh White (2002). This book was written for parents and professionals about young children with autistic spectrum disorders, where the perspective of *that* child is considered when writing a story that will help develop the child's skills and concepts in particular social situations.

Can I Tell You about Asperger Syndrome: A Guide for Friends and Family, by Jude Welton (2002). This book was written specifically for the age group 7–15 years to help them to understand the problems faced by other children with AS. It also benefits children and young people who have themselves received a diagnosis of AS.

Freaks, Geeks and Asperger Syndrome: A User Guide to Adolescence, by Luke Jackson (2002). Written by Luke when he was 13 years old, having been diagnosed with AS, this book was specifically aimed at sharing his knowledge with other adolescents with AS to help them to better understand their own condition.

An Asperger Marriage, by Gisela and Christopher Slater-Walker (2002). Here the authors write about the trials and tribulations of their relationship, and how their commitment to one another enabled them to find ways to overcome their difficulties and ultimately forge a successful marriage.

I found all of these books to be compelling reading and particularly relevant and informative when wanting to gain knowledge about people with AS in specific age groups and in various relationships. However, because other books are not mentioned does not imply that they are not as informative or useful, it merely means that I have faith in these books because I have read them and can recommend them accordingly.

Having suggested that reading books is one way of gaining knowledge about AS (I also make reference to articles and films later in the book), connecting with other people with AS via case studies is an effective way of understanding situations through identification. It is my hope that the various issues and problems outlined in the case studies referred to in this book will enable people in AS relationships to identify with their own difficulties. Some of the issues and problems presented may seem to match with the reader's almost exactly, whilst others may be similar enough to be able to relate to sufficiently well to be able to use the strategies in the format I recommend, or in a way that the reader can adapt to match their own specific needs.

Chapter 2

Stage Two:
Individual Counselling

*Over one's mind and over one's body
the individual is sovereign.*

John Stuart Mill

In any healthy relationship between partners a balance needs to be maintained between the autonomy necessary for each to be their own person, and the intimacy that each needs to feel an equal and wanted member of that partnership. This can be tricky to achieve at the best of times in the best of relationships, but it can be especially trying in an Asperger relationship where the AS partner is likely to experience great difficulty in understanding the emotional and social needs of their NT mate.

Where the wants of the NT partner may not have been heard, seemingly not understood and certainly not acted upon in this relationship, it is crucial when entering the counselling process that this partner be given the opportunity to express those wants and to have them heard and acknowledged on a one-to-one basis by the therapist undertaking the counselling. Providing this opportunity in this way may be the first time the NT partner has had the experience of being listened to since their marriage or partnership began.

However, having this opportunity also applies to the AS partner, for it is often the case in conjoint counselling that he or she will say what they believe their NT partner wants to hear in order to avoid conflict, and so they are just as unlikely to express their own wants and concerns. It is for this reason that initial counselling should be separate for both partners so that their own needs can be understood before co-counselling commences, and should remain an option later on in the process.

Historically, it was the case that Relate held the 'couple' or the 'relationship' to be the client, but in the 60 years since the organisation was created, much has changed. In keeping with changes in society and many recent Acts of Parliament that impact directly upon the family as an institution and also the world of counselling and therapeutic interventions, Relate no longer views the 'couple' or the 'relationship' to be the client, but rather the individuals within that relationship. This revised stance was formalised by Relate in July 2006 in a document entitled *Who is the Client?*, which now entitles counsellors to see clients who are in a relationship individually.

The importance of this option in the counselling process was expressed by several of the interviewees in my research and has been built into my counselling model accordingly. How each partner genuinely feels about the relationship, as individually expressed in Stage Two, can be shared in the relative safety of the therapist when co-counselling commences.

In all cases when I see clients separately, I explore three specific aspects of their relationship. The first is 'Attraction', where I ask what was attractive about their partner when they first met and courted; what was it that made this person special enough to want to be in a relationship with? The next is 'Issues' as I try to discover what has changed in the relationship for the clients and what are their concerns? The third aspect is 'Wants', from this I seek to understand what the client wants for the relationship that the counselling process might provide. In this way I bring the clients from their past to their present in relational terms, but also offer them an opportunity to think about and express what their future might look like.

It is at this time that I want to introduce you to the couples in the case studies referred to in Chapter 1. There are four of them, and whilst their identities have been changed to ensure confidentiality is maintained, the relationship issues described in the case studies are real.

Case study 1 – Anne and Bob
A brief history

At the time of coming to see me, Anne was 56 years of age and Bob was 55. Both had been married before and had grown up children. They had been married to one another for six years. Anne worked part-time in a supermarket, whilst Bob worked as a counter assistant in a builder's merchant. At a time when Anne was experiencing difficulties in their marriage (Bob didn't realise there was anything wrong), she read a newspaper article about AS and immediately recognised aspects of Bob's behaviour. She shared it with him and he accepted that certain elements of the behaviour in the article related to him. He subsequently saw his GP who referred him to a psychologist who formally diagnosed him with AS.

Individual interview with Anne

Attraction: Anne was attracted to Bob because he was quiet and unassuming, kind and gentle. He was also very intelligent, which appealed to Anne. Although not outgoing in general terms, he was good company and had a witty sense of humour. He was different from other men that Anne had met in that he seemed more responsible and reliable.

Issues: Bob was very attentive to Anne when they first met and he doted on her, sometimes to the point where she felt overwhelmed by it. However, since their marriage, and particularly in the two years preceding counselling, Anne began to feel distanced from Bob, and isolated and excluded by him. This was accompanied by a lack of intimacy in the relationship and love-making was now rare. Even kissing and cuddling seemed to be an effort for him. Anne described their relationship as being one-sided, with all the affection and effort coming from her. Bob's behaviour seemed to be defined more and more by routines and things having to be done his way.

Wants: Anne stated that she wanted Bob to be there for her and for her not to feel as if she was having to carry all the burdens of the marriage on her own. She wanted him to share his feelings and thoughts with her and for him to be less 'robotic'. She wanted to feel as if their relationship was on 'their' terms instead of 'his'.

Individual interview with Bob

Attraction: Bob had found Anne to be 'very nice looking' when they first met and he didn't feel challenged or threatened by her personality; she was easy to get on with. He felt that they enjoyed the same interests, which were largely music, reading and sometimes going to the cinema.

Issues: In accepting his behaviour was different from other men, Bob said he had always felt different, even recalling his childhood and recognising his dissimilarity to the other boys in his class. He went on to describe himself as being very rule-bound and said, 'I wouldn't break a rule even if nobody would know about it.' He said he felt happier working in a structured way and routines helped him achieve this. Bob said that Anne would regularly ask him if he was feeling ok and if everything was alright. Most of the time everything was fine and so he would get annoyed with Anne for asking him this. On those occasions when he wasn't feeling ok, he would normally respond, 'No, I'm fine,' because he didn't know why he was feeling the way he was and how to express this to Anne.

Wants: Bob said he wanted to be able to communicate better with Anne (possibly by writing things down) and to be able to give her more support. He said, 'All I want is for me and my wife to get on better than we do now.'

Case study 2 – Barbara and Chris
A brief history

Sixty-two-year-old Barbara was a retired librarian, whilst Chris, aged 65, was a retired master builder. They had been married for 44 years and had a son aged 39 and a daughter aged 32. Retirement was a culture shock for both partners, but particularly so for Barbara. She stated that because Chris had for many years worked away on large building contracts (only coming home every other weekend at times), she felt their new-found relationship was akin to that of Victor and Margaret Meldrew in the television series *One Foot in the Grave*. Although Barbara felt that she and Chris had never really communicated at an emotional level, she now felt he was almost a stranger. This wasn't the man she had married 44 years earlier! Being a well-read person, Barbara had heard about AS and obtained various articles about it. Having read the articles, her conclusion was they could have been written about Chris. He came along to counselling at her request and with an open mind.

Individual interview with Barbara

Attraction: When Barbara first met Chris she found him to be a polite, unassuming man. She respected the fact that he was direct when expressing his views about things, but he wasn't forceful about them. Chris wasn't 'one-of-the-lads'; rather he was a quiet, intellectual person that she just enjoyed being with.

Issues: Chris had never been overly communicative but, since coming together in retirement, Barbara found his behaviour to be odd. There was little real communication between them and misunderstandings were common with regard to what they were doing or where they were going. His former direct way of expressing himself had now changed, now when he spoke to her it often felt like he was being boorish. She couldn't understand how such an intelligent man could do things so differently from what seemed to her to be the obvious way of doing them. When she challenged him about why he did things the way he did, he would ask, 'Can you write it down for me so I can consider it?'

Wants: Barbara's needs from counselling were straightforward, she simply wanted communication to improve between her and Chris so they could be more of a couple in their twilight years.

Individual interview with Chris

Attraction: Chris liked Barbara because she had a quiet personality that he felt suited his. He knew that as a librarian she was intelligent and liked reading, which was one of his hobbies also. They used to do crossword puzzles together as another shared hobby. Chris had been surprised that Barbara had taken to him as he thought she was very pretty, but he saw himself as quite ordinary.

Issues: Communicating emotional or sensitive things had always been difficult for Chris and it hadn't got any easier over the course of time. He said that one of the benefits of working away a lot was that he wasn't placed in situations where he had to be expressive at an emotional level. He stated he knew he did things differently from Barbara, but to him it seemed as if he was doing things in a logical fashion and he didn't understand why she would think otherwise.

Wants: Chris wasn't sure why things weren't very good between him and Barbara, he just knew they weren't. He said he wanted to learn to work with Barbara on overcoming what he described as their times of tension. Asked to explain what a 'time of tension' was, he said, 'It's all about communication, I just want it to be better.'

Case study 3 – Carol and Doug
A brief history

Carol, a 34-year-old ex-nurse, was married to Doug, a 33-year-old fireman. They had been married for three years and had a daughter, aged 18 months. When a mutual friend had introduced them on a blind date, Carol was immediately smitten by Doug's seemingly confident, outgoing personality. Whilst their courtship days were memorable for all the right reasons, things changed quite dramatically and quickly after they were married and Carol became pregnant. It was when working as a nurse that Carol first heard of AS and, based on her instincts in linking this recollected knowledge with Doug's behaviour, she started exploring AS on the Internet as well as buying Gisela and Christopher Slater-Walker's book *An Asperger Marriage*. In her mind this told her all she needed to know about Doug's changed behaviour. He was initially resistant to the idea of having AS, but subsequently agreed to a diagnosis, which was positive.

Individual interview with Carol

Attraction: From the first time that Carol met Doug she was not only struck by his confident, self-assured disposition, she also thought him very handsome with an impressive physique (as a fireman he had to maintain a high level of physical fitness). Because of her bad experiences in a previous relationship, Carol saw Doug as a breath of fresh air and as her 'knight in shining armour'.

Issues: Carol saw a change in Doug almost immediately they married and started living together. It was as if he knew how to fulfil the role of someone involved in courtship and how to engage with the 'rules' of that process, but he didn't know how to fulfil the role of a husband or understand what being a husband was about. This situation became exacerbated when Carol fell pregnant and she became more reliant on Doug for moral and physical support as the pregnancy advanced. When their baby daughter was born, Carol described Doug as being totally inept and clueless in his now combined roles of husband and father.

Wants: Above all else, Carol wanted Doug to be a positive influence in her life. She hoped that the current situation was simply because Doug did not understand what being a husband and a father was all about and that he could learn these roles and also the rules around sharing and communicating at an intimate level, conducive to being in a committed relationship.

Individual interview with Doug

Attraction: Before meeting Carol, Doug had not had many girlfriends (something that surprised Carol when this became known to her) and he was flattered by the fact that she was attracted to him. He thought her pretty, with a bubbly personality, and he was struck by how kind she was and how comfortable he felt in her company. He enjoyed their courtship very much and found he could easily balance his professional life as a fireman with his social life as Carol's boyfriend.

Issues: Despite his seemingly gregarious nature, Doug said he had always been shy and was easily embarrassed in the presence of women of his age group. Carol was different though, she reminded him a bit of his mother and he thought this probably contributed to how easily they got on together. However, when they married, he felt that much more was expected of him and he wasn't sure how to react to these expectations. At first he stumbled his way through, not sure of what to do in various circumstances, but feeling that he was doing his best. However, it always seemed to him that whatever he did was never enough for Carol and by the time they came to see me for couple therapy, Doug felt he was being constantly criticised and that Carol didn't give him credit for contributing in any way to their family life other than him being the 'bread-winner'.

Wants: Doug wanted things to be as they were between him and Carol when they first started going out together. He realised that they had to be different in some ways because they now had a young daughter, but he just wanted the three of them to be happy together and for Carol to feel he was supportive of her. The current situation in the relationship was making him feel depressed and he couldn't understand what was making him such a 'bad' husband, albeit he accepted that he had difficulty empathising with Carol's needs in certain situations (e.g. when she was pregnant and during childbirth). It was his desire for the relationship to be happy again that prompted him to agree to go for the AS diagnosis and to attend couple counselling.

Case study 4 – Diane and Eric
A brief history

Forty-one-year-old Diane and 47-year-old Eric had been married for ten years when they came to see me for couple therapy. They had a daughter aged one at this time. Although not initially noticeable, some of Eric's behaviour (particularly after their daughter was born) gave Diane cause for concern. It was after she had read about AS that she believed she could identify it in Eric. It was discussed between them and although he was accepting of being the subject of certain AS issues, he was disinclined to attend counselling at that time. She was, however, relieved that he wanted to save their marriage. It was agreed that counselling would initially be for Diane, but with the hope that Eric would attend later, which he did.

Individual interview with Diane

Attraction: Diane told me that she was initially attracted to Eric because he was a gentleman; well mannered and nicely spoken. She felt he had a totally different way about him and that he was unlike any other man she had ever met. She described him as being 'innocent', a quality that she had never experienced in any other man. She also described Eric as being 'isolated' which induced in her a desire to want to accompany him in that world.

Issues: For Diane, she first noticed Eric's routines when they started living together before they got married. In her eyes he became more inflexible after their daughter was born. She accepted that sometimes her own behaviour was inappropriate and that she lost her temper with him in a way she described as 'furious and aggressive', but felt this was born purely out of her frustration with the situation. Diane was very concerned about the effect of hers and Eric's relationship upon their daughter. On one occasion when she had broached the issue of AS with Eric, he reacted defensively and said that talking to him about AS issues was like 'pouring petrol on the embers of a fire'. Yet on other occasions he identified with having AS traits, but attributed them to a side of him that he didn't know.

Wants: Diane's needs from counselling were primarily to save their marriage, but in the course of so doing to make her relationship with Eric more stable and more communicative. She also wanted to have a better understanding of her husband from his perspective, and hoped that all of these improvements would benefit their daughter.

Individual interview with Eric

Attraction: Having met Diane via a choir group, Eric immediately felt he could identify with her. Their conjoint singing activities and other shared mutual interests made for a comfortable and meaningful union as far as he was concerned.

Issues: Eric said that Diane had always been a bit bossy, but after their daughter was born, he felt she became more aggressive and domineering, whilst at the same time he began to feel irrelevant. He felt he had to stand up to Diane in order to be able to assert his views. He said it felt to him that their relationship took one step forwards and ten back and he went on to make an analogy between poor dental hygiene and the 'decaying' behaviour that remained untreated and was disrupting their family system.

Wants: Stability in their relationship was the first need that Eric expressed, allied to not having to 'tread on eggshells' when talking to Diane or even just being in her company. He also wanted to feel that he counted for something in the relationship as opposed to feeling he was an outsider, something he had been feeling ever since their daughter had been born.

So there we have them, the eight individual interviews of my case study clients in accordance with Stage Two of my counselling model. Having already stated the advantages of this process with regard to each client feeling they have been given the opportunity to have their voice heard and to be able to express their feelings and concerns in the absence of their partner, I feel this stage serves another very important function, that of each client being able to feel that they have an understanding and the beginnings of their own trusting relationship with the counsellor.

Try as one may, it is sometimes very difficult for a counsellor to remain entirely impartial during the counselling process, and even if one can manage to achieve this at a conscious level, there is still the possibility of unconsciously favouring one client over the other. For my own part, I am very aware in my practice that there is a client in the room (more commonly the male partner) that has AS or displays AS traits and that I will usually be able to identify easily with him in that regard. I also have to be aware that if I am dealing with a heterosexual couple, then I am one of two men in the room and that the female partner may feel threatened or compromised by this. Link these two features together and the NT female partner may be doubly disadvantaged by being in the counselling room with two men with AS.

Individual counselling of itself will never take this potential away, but it can serve to raise the counsellor's awareness of his or her relationship with each client as an individual, as opposed to thinking of the 'relationship' between the couple as the client. I find that if I can succeed in remaining aware of these issues at a conscious level, there is little opportunity (or at least it is significantly reduced) for me to become biased towards or against either client at an unconscious level. Individual counselling, within the context of the whole model, can therefore serve to positively influence the clients by giving them a sense of 'self' during therapy and enhance their potential to engage with the counsellor, and it can benefit the counsellor by creating a stronger therapeutic alliance with the clients and thereby better prepare them for developing and working with the strategies and tasks that come later in the counselling process.

Chapter 3

Stage Three: Co-Counselling Begins

After all these years, I see that I was mistaken about
Eve in the beginning; it is better to live outside the
Garden with her than inside it without her.

Mark Twain

Statistics reveal there is a 9:1 ratio of men over women being diagnosed with AS. Sometimes such a diagnosis can be like a beacon of light for the person who personally endures it, as it helps him make sense of the trials and tribulations he has experienced through life; the failed friendships, the bullying, the sense of difference, the isolation and the lack of intimacy. It can also bring great relief to the female partner who may have wondered over the years why the man she fell in love with has treated her in a way that has been anything but loving and considerate. It has often been the case, within my experience, that a wife or female partner has believed that such seemingly cruel treatment from her AS partner had been directed at her as a punishment because she had not been a good enough partner, and on this basis she has assumed that his behaviour was justified. Imagine then her relief, possibly after living under such a misapprehension for many years, to discover that her spouse's treatment of her was not intended to be unkind or malicious and that she had, indeed, been a good other-half in their relationship. I recall one such female client saying to me, 'Our courtship was a lovely time, but it was only when we married and started living together that I began feeling distanced and excluded from my husband. That was 30 years ago and I've been dogged all that time by the feeling that I wasn't a good enough wife. Only since we've been seeing you have I come to know that it wasn't me and it wasn't him – it was Asperger Syndrome.' But a diagnosis can also be distressing news for the NT partner when she initially accepts and welcomes this news, but then despairs as she learns that AS has no cure and she may only be subjected to more of the same behaviour from her AS partner.

There are variations of acceptance and non-acceptance of this condition by each of the partners. Where they both come to learn of his likelihood of having AS (by whatever means) and are accepting of it, the situation lends itself to the counselling process as both partners are 'on the same side', so to speak. Problems are more likely to occur where, for example, she has read something about AS and tries to share this with him in the hope of him accepting her 'diagnosis', but he is resolute in rejecting her findings, feeling that the blame for the demise of the relationship is being placed firmly on his shoulders. The relationship, at this point, is likely to deteriorate even more.

I have also had the experience where a male partner came to know about AS and recognised it in himself, and then attempted to share this belief with his wife. It was then the wife who was the rejecting one because she had seen him act in an apparently 'normal' way with other people and could not understand or accept why he could not act the same way with her. What she wouldn't have known was that his behaviour with others was most likely to be adapted, such that he consciously tried and very often succeeded in blending in by taking on the characteristics of the people he was with at that time. In this way he hoped to fit in and be accepted by that particular set of people. The difference when he was with his wife was that he consciously didn't want to be anyone else; he wanted to be accepted by her for being the person that he was. It was after this experience that the partners came to see me for Asperger counselling and these issues were explored and understood. The *chameleon effect*, as I refer to it, often goes unnoticed by the people who are being 'copied' as they are more than welcoming of anyone who appears to share their own views and general way of being and, in any event, such interactions are usually short-lived. It is those who are intimately connected to these chameleon-like people and know them at close quarters who struggle to understand this phenomenon as they bear witness to the various changes in behaviour that come about when they are in the company of different people.

Whatever the balance of acceptance by the partners regarding one of them having AS, this will undoubtedly impact upon their ability as a couple both to positively influence the therapy they are entering into and in turn be positively influenced by it.

Whilst the previous chapter was devoted to understanding the clients as individuals, and as hearing them express their own views on the three significant aspects of what attracted each to the other; how and when their problems came about and what they each want for the future of the relationship, this chapter is about bringing those views together and sharing them in the containing space of the counselling room and under the stewardship of the counsellor. It isn't necessary for the clients to agree about their problems at this stage (I would suggest this is almost impossible without a much deeper knowledge of AS), but it is important for them to begin to acknowledge that they will have different perspectives on these problems. In effect, the sharing of views tells each partner how the other feels about everything and helps to set the scene for how the counselling will continue. For example, in one relationship both partners may earnestly want their marriage to continue and for their problems to be resolved to their mutual satisfaction, and there will be a great sense of positivity derived from them both knowing this. Whilst in another relationship, one of the partners (usually the NT partner) may be totally disillusioned or angry or depressed (or all three) about the way she sees her husband or partner react to her, their children and their friends, to the point that she can see no future for them together. The other partner, however, (usually the one with AS) fails to understand what all the fuss and commotion is about. In cases such as this there will be little positivity, much uncertainty and probably little hope. My own sense of hope on these occasions is bolstered because the clients have not just sat back and watched their relationship slip away; they have taken that first important step to try and understand what went wrong and to change things – they have entered the counselling room, and once the clients have done this then anything is potentially possible.

Importantly, this chapter is also about helping the clients develop a conjoint understanding, at a basic level initially, of what AS is and what potential it has to impact negatively upon their relationship. So as not to be entirely negative, it is also right to say that there can be positive impacts upon relationships once the differences between the Asperger mind and the neuro-typical mind are better understood and awareness of AS is raised. I discussed in Chapter 1 the merits of reading when it comes to gaining knowledge, and once again reading takes a primary role in this next stage of counselling.

I have been fortunate in gathering together what, in my view, are some very interesting and insightful articles about AS (beyond the reading that I have previously recommended). Whilst certain of these articles relate to the many problems experienced by couples within relationships and by those that are emotionally or intimately connected to them, one article in particular is taken from the perspective of an individual who is not in a relationship as a spouse or partner, but accepts through his description of his childhood, adolescence and early adult years that he is both challenging and very wearing to live with. It is my practice with my clients to invite them to read four of these articles. The articles are not lengthy and therefore not too challenging, particularly for someone who may not yet be prepared to accept that he even has AS. The whole point in asking my clients to undertake the reading is for them to see what, if anything, each of them can respectively identify with in terms of attitudes, behaviour and relationship problems. I also ask them to make notes of what elements of the reading they are able to identify with, and for them to bring these notes with them to the next counselling session for us to have some discussion around. I specifically suggest that they don't discuss with one another their respective views before coming to counselling as it is my intention to help them to develop a conjoint understanding of AS and of each other's perspective of it (where the AS mind allows this). It is not about giving the clients further ammunition for arguing before counselling even properly commences!

The first of these articles is taken from *Woman's Weekly* magazine, dated September 2003, and is entitled 'At Last You Can Say I Love You'. It takes the form of a letter from Gisela Slater-Walker to her husband, Chris (you will recall that I mentioned their book *An Asperger Marriage* in Chapter 1 as recommended reading), in which she describes to him their relationship from when they met until the time she penned this letter. The useful thing about this account is that it seems so ordinary, from how they first met as students at Manchester University whilst doing the same course, how they shared common interests such as classical music and how they became drawn to one another. Up until this point, this letter could relate to any of thousands of couples that have embarked on courtship and subsequent marriage.

Gisela goes on, however, to describe the little things she first noticed about Chris that were different; he was shy, socially reluctant and awkward, as well as often tactless. But as with other AS couples, Gisela found some of his ways strangely attractive. It was when Chris started living with Gisela and her three children from her first marriage that their communication problems really came to the fore. Despite marrying four years later, the issues around Chris being seemingly thoughtless towards Gisela and she thinking he was being manipulative came to a head and communication between them deteriorated to the point of a brief separation. It was only after they were reunited and watching television one evening that a programme was screened about AS. Gisela and Chris immediately recognised many of the issues as appertaining to them. His subsequent diagnosis via the National Autistic Society was a changing point in their lives. Gisela concludes her letter to Chris by praising him for the effort he makes in the areas of socialising and communicating that he ordinarily finds so difficult. Now he even tells Gisela he loves her – by e-mail.

This is such a case as I alluded to earlier where both partners were accepting of the AS situation that confronted them and were thereby more easily able to work together to overcome their problems. One of my client couples experienced similar problems to Gisela and Chris (as outlined in this article) for over 20 years, and was immensely relieved to be able to attribute them to AS after he willingly received a positive diagnosis. The female client said of this article, 'I can so easily identify with Gisela's frustrations because Pete (pseudonym) could be sincere and warm sometimes, but then totally lacking in empathy at other times. I actually wondered if he wasn't schizophrenic.' Her AS husband (Pete) said in response to reading this article, 'I can very much identify with the social awkwardness expressed and described in this article. Relationships are very hard for me to initiate and maintain and I'm always very anxious about saying the wrong thing.'

The second article is from *Life on Saturday Magazine* (2001) and is 'Why Won't He Talk To Me?' by Lucy Miller. This article is a bit more direct and gets straight to the point about the Asperger partner's obsessions, rituals and fixed interests and how these very often shape the relationship. It continues by mentioning work undertaken by the National Autistic Society (current at that time) that suggests that almost half of the people who have the AS condition are not diagnosed with it until they are in their adult years. It also stresses that many other people do not know they have it.

Lest you think this article is one that is altogether too depressing to give my clients to read, it is not without hope. Indeed, it goes on to quote the experiences of two particular families, where the problems of each family are briefly outlined, as are some of the compromises, arrangements and strategies they have put in place as an outcome of their raised awareness, and from which they have ultimately benefited.

In response to this article, one male client said, 'I've always had difficulty communicating, even with people I've known for years. I'm never sure what I say to people is the right thing to say and if I get it wrong it puts me off trying again. I've lost contact with lots of friends because of this. Now we know about Asperger Syndrome, we work together at what I might say to people. I still get it wrong sometimes, but now I know why.' Another male client said, 'It mentions in this article about wives needing a hug, mine insists on having a hug every day, but I just don't get it; I don't see the importance of them. I've always been thought of as a bit unconventional ever since I was at junior school, but articles like this make me realise there are others like me who have made changes for the better.' One of my female clients read this article and said, 'We've had so many problems over the years, but now we know it's his AS. We've both said how unfair it is that we didn't know about this years ago, and if we had things could have been so different. We've lost a lot of time, but at least now we can work together for a better future.' And finally, this response came from another female client of mine, 'I've always felt he puts less effort into our relationship than I do and he seems to get on better with other people than with me. It has been difficult at times to remain in this relationship, but I can understand more now about the way he thinks and behaves.'

If any of the four articles is likely to really challenge the clients (particularly the AS partner) to tell it how it is in their relationship, then it will be this next one. 'The Truth is I'm Exhausting to Live With' was written by Nicholas Barrow and published in the *Guardian* in May 2004. Of all the various articles I've read this is the one that I can most easily identify with, particularly when Nicholas talks of his early years and the fixed routines, the precise attention to detail and the brutal destruction of items, objects and basically anything if they didn't work according to how he thought they should. Even though I am much less 'fixed' in my own ways now and my obsessive compulsive disorder (OCD) is measurably more manageable, my wife still sees many similarities between Nicholas in his adult years and me in mine!

The reason I suggest that this is the most challenging of the articles is that it's the most intense. It outlines behaviour that is more extreme than that described in the other articles, or at least describes it in a more graphic way. For example, from the age of six Nicholas had been obsessed with recording chart music from the radio. He created an enormous collection of tapes, each of which was labelled very precisely and then placed in an exact order. At 13 years of age Nicholas would polish the covers of his CD collection with Windolene and be intensely upset if any of the covers became scratched (one can only imagine his upset if one of the CDs became damaged). Having been formally diagnosed with AS, Nicholas spent much of his youth in a boarding school for special needs children. Some of the children he met there were violent and he was often bullied. If one of them hit Nicholas, he would get very angry and often cause damage in one of the school rooms and have to be restrained. He would then sulk for several days before hitting the 'offender' back when he wasn't looking!

Even though his anger and violence stopped when he was 16 years old, he is still very organised and gets upset by things being untidy. In his own words Nicholas says, 'The truth is I am absolutely exhausting to live with.' Nicholas now lives a semi-independent life in a house overseen by professional staff trained in autistic spectrum disorders. So you can see it would require brutal honesty as well as courage on the part of the NT spouse in describing her AS partner in anything akin to this way, simply on the basis that he may feel insulted or vilified by such a description and be totally unforgiving of her for so doing. However, the following comments were made by some of my female clients about their potentially AS partners:

> Client A: 'I can see a lot of my husband in this article, the obsessive collecting of things – most of which have no earthly use – being very tidy and domesticated, and getting enraged about things that to me don't seem to be that important. He definitely has been exhausting to live with over the years and sometimes just impossible!'

Client B: 'My husband is a bit like Nicholas Barrow in that he has an obsessive need to know how something works to the point of reducing it into little bits and then not being able to put it back together again. He also tries to fix things when they go wrong and then invalidates the warranty. It drives me mad because we often have to buy replacement items when there is no need to.'

It also takes a great deal of acceptance on the part of the AS partner to acknowledge that his behaviour, or some of it at least, is on the scale of behaviour that Nicholas Barrow describes. One male client went as far as saying, 'I'm a bit like Nicholas in that if one of my cassette tape boxes gets damaged then I have to replace it, which is difficult nowadays as the shops sell mostly CDs. But even so, I'm most certainly not as extreme as him in other ways.' Another male client simply responded to this article by saying, 'I am definitely not as bad as the man in that article – no way!'

The fourth and final article I offer to my clients is called 'My Darling Stranger', published in *The Times* on 16 February 2002. It takes us back again to the marriage of Gisela and Christopher Slater-Walker, but in much greater detail. The relationship between Gisela and Christopher is explained via an interview of the couple at their home by the author of the article, Valerie Grove. During her time with the couple, Valerie noticed that Christopher showed her courtesy by taking her coat and holding the door open for her, as well as smiling and making eye contact with her, but these things do not come naturally to Chris, they are all learned social graces, taught to him in the most part by Gisela. In addition to these learned skills, he also has to rehearse what he might say during the course of a conversation with anyone, in this instance Valerie.

Gisela explains in this interview that Chris doesn't engage easily in verbal communication because he doesn't understand the finer points of taking turns, or not talking too long before letting the other person speak. He doesn't understand or acknowledge the intricacies of non-verbal signals such as nodding or making utterances such as 'Oh' or 'Mmm' that tell people that you are paying attention to what they are saying. Later in the interview Chris explains to Valerie how at the age of 31 he was formally diagnosed with AS and how this then made sense of his life for him, of why he had felt a sense of angst about life in general ever since he could remember. He went on to say that he had felt distanced from the world at large and what was going on in it, but he also felt threatened by it.

Even when Chris left boarding school and went to Manchester University he was self-conscious, insular, melancholic and anti-social, if not all of the time then most of it. He was more than a bit surprised when an attractive woman in the shape of Gisela started to show an interest in him. The interview continues by describing how their relationship evolved through their conjoint interests and their spiritual and intellectual connectedness, but it also explains the development of the relational problems they suffered through Chris's inability to express affection or to even give compliments to Gisela. It was only after Chris's diagnosis that these things made sense to them.

This article gives a different account of how Gisela and Chris came to know about AS. In this version Gisela's brother-in-law gave her a book called *An Anthropologist on Mars* that recounted (in part) the story of Temple Grandin, a world-renowned author on autistic spectrum disorders who has herself been diagnosed with autism. It was from this description of Temple Grandin that Gisela recognised many of Chris's characteristics. The remainder of this article gives a detailed account of how they gained an in-depth awareness of what AS is about and how, with much effort on the part of Chris and with enduring patience and fortitude on the part of Gisela, they got their marriage back on track.

This is the longest and most detailed of the articles and gives greater clarity (in my view) as to how the various AS traits can impact upon a relationship. I think it's for this reason that my male clients can more easily see aspects of themselves in the article. One male client said, 'I can identify with having a lack of social graces, albeit I am, according to my wife, better than I used to be. I certainly know what it's like to feel a universal angst about everything – I always have and I still do, particularly in the presence of other people.' Another male client wrote this response: 'I can relate to a lot of what Chris says and does in this article. I too feel compelled to fulfil non-functional routines in that I can't tolerate seeing tea-towels, table-cloths or any other such things all scrunched up – they have to be either hanging perfectly straight or laid perfectly flat. Also, if Mary says something out of anger or frustration to get a response from me, I don't know how to deal with it and so I just look at her.' A female client of mine said of this article, 'Unlike Chris, Jim does tell me he loves me, but I believe he says it now because he knows I want to hear it. Saying "I love you" doesn't come naturally to Jim, I feel it is a learnt response from him. Sometimes, if I'm feeling needy and ask him if he loves me, he will say, "I told you I did last week, why are you asking me again?"'

You might ask me, 'Why give these particular articles to your clients as opposed to more recent ones?' My answer is simple; whilst they may date from between 2001 to 2004, these articles give a balance of the more rigid appliance to rituals as seen through the eyes of Nicholas Barrow, the sense of universal angst and sense of threat experienced by Chris Slater-Walker, and the sheer frustration, anger and upset felt by his wife, Gisela, in their pre-diagnosis days. To date, having read many other articles, I have not found any that give a more comprehensive account of how AS can affect relationships in so many ways. It is to this end that I give my clients the stories of these people who have been brave enough to write about how

AS has affected their lives, because I believe that there is something in these stories as a collection that most people in an AS relationship can identify with.

I want to mention briefly the use of DVD and video material that can also provide a useful insight into the problems of AS relationships. There is, however, an issue I need to address immediately in that whilst publications of newspaper or magazine articles are generally quite easy to obtain without any legal complications (although it is illegal to copy newspaper articles without permission except for personal use), the use of DVD and video material is governed by laws relating to copyright and I am not at liberty to simply copy extracts of videos that I might supply to clients without falling foul of this legislation. That said, I am able to suggest certain titles that my clients may wish to purchase for themselves, or alternatively I can loan them others that I do have at my disposal.

There are many DVDs and videos available on the subject of AS, but most seem to be directed towards AS children and how their parents, teachers and other professionals can assist them in life. Whilst this is admirable and very necessary, it is apparent that there are not many DVDs or videos that deal with adults with AS, particularly those in relationships. Where they do exist, they are often only available in the United States (and only usable on US standard equipment) or they are of very short duration (some as short as 14 minutes) and therefore very expensive.

That said, there are some very good short films available on DVD and videos from the National Autistic Society that are both appropriate to adults and not overly expensive, and there are three in particular I would like to recommend:

- *Outside In: Living with Asperger Syndrome* This is a 20-minute DVD that spotlights three men with AS who talk about their anxieties from their respective points of view. They also talk about their particular interests and the implications of these on their relationships.

- *Whichever Way You Look at It, It's Still Autism* This runs for 30 minutes and is the story of Larry Arnold a man with AS, who gives his views on life from an autistic perspective.

- *Asperger Syndrome: A Different Mind* This 29-minute DVD includes the accounts of adults and children as they talk about the problems they confront at home, work and school and how they have faced them. What I like about this film is its broad approach to three different environments from the minds of adults and children, providing a kind of history lesson for neurotypical spouses who may be able to identify better with their Asperger partner's problems reaching back to childhood.

There are also films available on general release that I would suggest are worthy of viewing, each for different but equally valid reasons. The first of these was released as recently as 2006 and is called *Snow Cake*. This is the story of an Englishman in Canada who has a motor accident in which his 19-year-old female hitch-hiker passenger is killed. The Englishman feels compelled to visit the young woman's mother whom he subsequently discovers has high-functioning autism. It is the relationship between these two principal characters that provides the thrust of the film.

Mozart And The Whale (2005) is a fictional account of a man and a woman, both of whom have AS. It is the story of how they came to know one another and develop a relationship. The male partner in this film is the one more obviously affected by AS, but the issues and problems of both characters and how they deal with them in the context of their relationship is what the film is about. It is loosely based on a real-life couple, the man having an intense interest in whales and his wife having savant skills whereby she can compose music and create intricate art forms simultaneously.

The third film I would recommend is called *As Good As It Gets (1997)*. The main character in this romantic comedy is a fiercely independent man with no friends, obsessive-compulsive routines and exacting expectations of other people. Whilst he is not outwardly described in the film as having either AS or high-functioning autism, the parallels (whether by accident or design) between his personality characteristics and those of a man with an autistic spectrum disorder are significant. Although the film is described as a comedy, it nonetheless depicts a very real and moving account of the main character's problems in the areas of human relationships.

In terms of raising awareness in order so that one can more easily identify with problem issues in one's own AS relationship, the articles, short films (DVD or video) and feature films that I have discussed here give a broad spectrum of relational problems and the concerns and frustrations of the individuals within those relationships. It has been my experience as an Asperger Counsellor using my counselling model that my clients have benefited from either reading these articles or viewing certain of the films, or both.

In the next chapter of this book, a general awareness of AS and the identification of its issues are further developed by exploring what aspects of the relationship the clients are in agreement about as being affected by AS (whether diagnosed or potential), and what aspects they disagree about, the latter being the ones that have more potential to damage the relationship.

Chapter 4

Stage Four: Acknowledging Different Perspectives

One ship sails East and another West by the self-same winds that blow, 'tis the set of the sails and not the gales that tells the way we go.

Ella Wheeler Wilcox

This stage of the model is all about generating a greater awareness of what AS is about by building on the reading and film materials used in the previous stage. My anticipated outcome for Stage Four is improved communication generally, but specifically by exploring the three areas of clarification, interpretation and translation. I will address each of these areas separately in due course, but first I want to clarify something with the reader that is an important prerequisite to any further counselling and is something I discuss earnestly with my clients.

It has been my experience that a lot of my male clients (the assumption being made that they are the AS partner) feel that they are either coming for therapy, or indeed being brought for therapy by their NT partner, on the basis that they are the one that has been pathologised as being 'ill' and therefore that therapy is an attempt to make them 'better'. Nothing could be further from the truth!

First, and let's not mince our words here, there is no cure for AS; it is a neurological difference in the way the brain is wired up, not something that can be caught like influenza and therefore simply remedied by medication, or a muscular pain that can be treated by physical manipulation of some kind. In her book *Pretending to Be Normal* Liane Holliday Willey states, 'Yet no matter the hardships, I do not wish for a cure to Asperger Syndrome. What I wish for is a cure for the common ill that pervades too many lives, the ill that makes people compare themselves to a normal that is measured in terms of perfect and absolute standards, most of which are impossible for anyone to reach' (Holliday Willey 1999, p.121). I agree wholeheartedly with this stance in making my second point, in that what I seek to achieve from the clients is an acknowledgement that their relationship is unique! It is like no other relationship because it cannot be. There may be similar personality characteristics to other people, habits and hobbies may be the same, lifestyles between two relationships may be alike and there may even be similar traits and problems of an AS nature between couples, but they are not the same because every individual within a relationship is just that, an individual, and every relationship is like a chemistry set where even the slightest difference in the ingredients makes for a different chemical compound, so there can be no such thing as a 'normal' way of being that people can compare themselves to.

It is this unique 'chemistry set' of a relationship that I have to impress upon the clients in terms of what they as individuals, warts and all, bring to the relationship, and so it does not benefit either partner to think in terms of only the AS partner being in need of a 'get well' remedy. It is about each partner being able to function fully as a person within that relationship, if this is what they want and are able to achieve, because if they cannot, then there is no relationship! On the question of 'Who is the client?' the perspective of National Relate has recently changed in line with the principles of justice and human rights. Their stance now is that the relationship is not the client, rather it is the individuals within the relationship who are the clients. I believe my own counselling doctrine accurately fits with that of Relate.

Having asked the partners to accept that their relationship is unique, what I also ask for at this time is some further acknowledgement that each of them is entitled to have their own views and opinions about the relationship and their part in it, and for them to be able to express those views in an appropriate way to one another. I try to impress upon each partner that they will have a view founded on their own belief system, based on how they were brought up, on their own emotional capabilities and so forth, and that there is no single 'truth' as to what is happening in their relationship, but rather multiple perspectives based on the 'product' that each of them is. Accordingly, I have developed a maxim that I present to clients in the form of a framed quote (Figure 4.1). Whilst I appreciate that this is sometimes a very difficult position for both partners to adopt, it is one that I ask them to consider from the outset. From a personal perspective, when I see things in a written format like this it assists me in taking new concepts on board, at least in the initial stages and until it becomes second nature. It is with this view in mind that I present my 'picture frame' maxim to my clients.

I want now to return to improving communication generally via the themes of clarification, interpretation and translation. But what do these

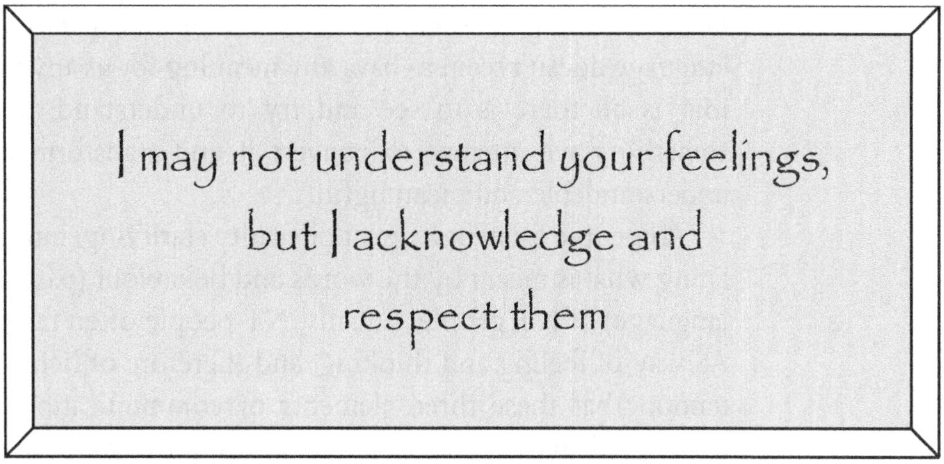

> I may not understand your feelings,
> but I acknowledge and
> respect them

Figure 4.1

terms mean? Couples come into the counselling room and when asked, 'What do you want from counselling?' the reply given as often as any other is 'We want to communicate better.' What do they mean? Do they speak a different language, do they not hear one another literally or metaphorically, do they speak acrimoniously to one another, or do they misinterpret and misunderstand one another? The word 'communicate' needs breaking down into more meaningful elements, and this is what I do in terms of clarifying, interpreting and translating how the clients speak to one another.

Clarification

To clarify something means to give to it the state or quality of being clear, particularly with reference to sounds or expressions, but it can just as easily apply to behaviour. When we clarify something we simplify it, we explain it and make it plain.

Interpretation

To interpret is to try to explain or bring out the meaning of words or behaviour. When we interpret something we construe it, we decipher it, we decode and define it.

Translation

To translate something is generally to express the sense of a word or sentence into a different language, and it is often said that AS people and NT people do speak a different 'language'. We often have to translate behaviour also, particularly when observing, for example, people with mental health problems who have little or no capacity to speak, or when language doesn't seem to have any meaning for us anymore and so behaviour is all there is to see and try to understand. When we translate something we attempt to convert it and transform it into something understandable and meaningful.

AS people often have great difficulty clarifying, interpreting and translating what is meant by the words and behaviour (particularly non-verbal language) of NT people. Equally, NT people often fail to understand the AS way of feeling and thinking, and therefore of behaving. It is my contention that these three elements of communication get progressively more difficult to undertake in accordance with the order that I've explained them. Clarification is the most straightforward practice to engage in; interpretation is arguably more involved and translation often needs the assistance of someone outside the relationship, such as a counsellor.

If we look again at some of my clients' responses to the articles I gave them to read in the previous chapter, we can place them in the context of the three elements of communication I have outlined and start to think about ways of addressing them. In response to one of the articles, one female client wrote, 'I've always felt he puts less effort into our relationship than I do.' The client is describing a feeling in this statement, something that is relatively tangible and in the normal course of things, something that partners in a relationship should be able to talk about and give clarity to. In an AS–NT relationship however, this may not be the case, but with practice the partners can learn to do so.

In describing her husband's behaviour relevant to a different article, another female client wrote, 'Saying "I love you" doesn't come naturally to Jim, I feel it is a learned response.' What the client did here was to create her own definition of what her husband might be feeling. She later told me she didn't think Jim knew what love was, but for fear of him perceiving it as criticism or a challenge, she hadn't checked it out with him. I did check it out with him and I'm sure he did know what love was, he just never knew the correct time or place to say it, and so rarely said it at all.

Another client wrote of her husband, 'I actually wondered if he wasn't schizophrenic.' This is a really powerful and worrying thing for a woman to think about the man she is married to and loves, but seemingly his words and deeds (or lack of them) were such that they couldn't be resolved by 'clarification' or 'interpretation'. This issue was a much deeper one that would probably take us to the other end of the communication spectrum and require a counsellor to help the clients to learn how to 'translate' such behaviour into something understandable.

In the course of generating a model for counselling couples in an AS–NT relationship, I had asked myself if there was a danger in asking them to read articles or watch films about other people's Asperger problems, especially given that I stress that no two couples are the same? Would I give them false hope if they read that a particular couple had achieved a better relationship by adopting a different way of doing something, or would I give them cause for despair if they read about Asperger problems and wondered, 'Is it going to get that bad?' However, the reality of being in an Asperger relationship is that it is a reality! Partners in a relationship are either willing to let things carry on as they are; willing to try to change things for the better or, if circumstances are such that neither of these ways seem possible, then serious consideration has to be given to ending the relationship. The answer to my own question is that the reality of AS in a relationship has to be faced but, in the course of facing this reality, the relationship of *that* couple has to be explored, understood and reacted to in ways that are idiosyncratic to their specific problems and how far they are prepared to go in addressing them.

As a way of demonstrating to my clients just how broad a spectrum Asperger Syndrome is, I show them a diagram that represents two AS

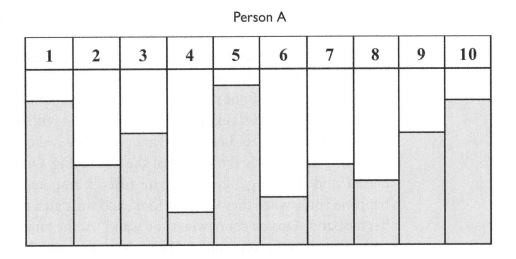

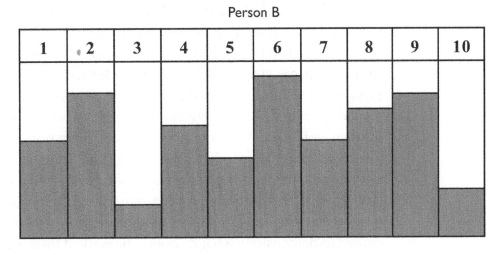

Figure 4.2

people, each of whom displays the same ten AS traits, but to different extents (Figure 4.2).

It might be, for example, that trait number 1 relates to a tendency to misinterpret words and phrases and to take them literally. I once said to one of my research subjects with regard to a certain issue, 'Where do you think you're wife is coming from on this?' His response, knowing that I was going to interview her later that day, was 'Home.' It will be seen from Figure 4.2 that Person A has a considerably higher potential to apply a literal meaning to things. Conversely, on trait number 4, which might relate to a lack of understanding of non-verbal language, it is Person B who has the higher potential to misunderstand or misinterpret. Finally, on trait number 10, which may apply to a limited understanding of emotional vocabulary, it is once again Person A who shows a lack of understanding at a higher level.

Imagine, then, meeting Person A and Person B and observing the apparent differences between them based on only ten traits. If we then build into the equation several more traits exhibited by a third person and more still by a fourth person, and then suggest that people with AS may have all or only a few of these traits and all at different degrees of intensity, we begin to understand just how complex an issue AS can be.

Although AS is a serious issue and can have grave implications for relationships, it should also be said that there can be humorous moments as well. I'm reminded of one such occasion in my counselling room when the female (NT) partner was explaining her frustration with her (AS) husband because it seemed to her that whenever they were out walking or shopping, he regularly ignored what she was saying. Only after repeating herself and rebuking him would he offer a response. I asked if this happened only when they were 'on foot', and she stated it did. I then asked her husband, 'Do you count when you walk?' At the same time as getting a look of total confusion from her, I also got a sheepish 'Yes' from him. She stated that she didn't understand why her husband would count as he walked along. I told her that it's all about things having to be regular and ordered. I said, 'If an AS person walks along the street and there are fence posts, the first few of which are five paces apart, they might expect them all to be five paces apart. It's the sort of order that AS people look for in everyday life.' She turned to him and asked, 'Do you do that?' To which he replied, 'Yes I do.' She answered him saying, 'No wonder you don't answer me then, you're too busy counting,' at which point both partners laughed. She asked me if I count when I walk along and I told her that I do it regularly. In pursuing the matter further I asked him, 'What do you do if it's obvious that the distance between two particular posts is going to be greater than the others?' At this point he got up from his seat and proceeded to demonstrate what he does – he walked three short paces across the room between two imaginary fence posts and then, as if realising that the second imaginary post could not be reached with another normal step, he took a much longer step in order to reach it. For those people familiar with the TV series 'Monty Python's Flying Circus', this was just like John Cleese doing his 'Ministry of Silly Walks' sketch. With a look of incredulity on her face his wife said, 'I've never seen you do that!' to which he replied, 'Well I'm not going to do it in front of you am I... I wait until you're looking the other way and then make up the longer step!' I drew an analogy for the couple with other people having a similar compulsion about not stepping on the cracks between paving slabs. The female partner asked me, 'Do you do that too?' I said, 'I don't have time to avoid the cracks, I'm too busy counting.'

Another funny moment occurred, again in my counselling room, when an AS client who is prone to having 'distant' moments, was struggling to be involved in the counselling session along with his wife and I. At this point I ought to explain that sometimes I show my clients a wedge-shaped diagram (Figure 4.3), which is a very simple neurological model of autistic spectrum disorders. The broader end of the wedge represents the more pronounced aspects of the spectrum and the narrow end represents the less severe aspects. The changes in shade in the vertical lines represent degrees of neurological change between various disorders.

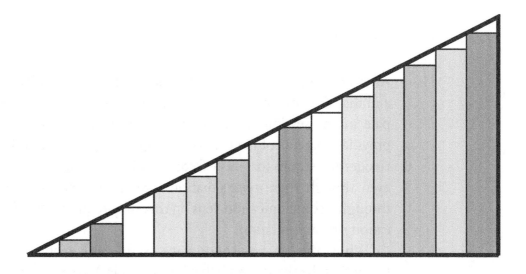

Figure 4.3: Neurological model of autistic spectrum disorders

This is of course, a very crude model, but it serves to make the point. On one occasion when I was drawing this on a flip chart for some clients, I had a lazy moment and rather than get out of my seat to draw, as I normally would, with my right hand, I leant over to my side and with my left hand and attempted to draw a rough sketch as per the neurological model shown above.

The outcome was approximate to that shown at Figure 4.4, which proved to be fit for purpose on that occasion. The dots in the narrow end of the wedge were my attempt to demonstrate that this is where most people with an autistic spectrum disorder (ASD) are situated. However, coming back to my male (AS) client who was having quite a prolonged 'distant' moment on the occasion under discussion, I asked him, 'Ian, your mind seems to be elsewhere, are you ok?' He replied, 'Why have you got a drawing of a parsnip behind you?'

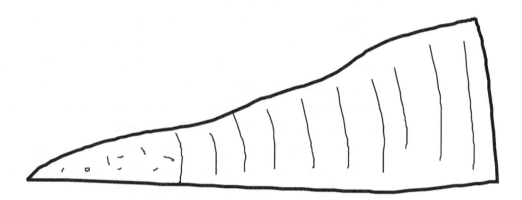

Figure 4.4

After I explained to him what it was, and that it was a left-handed sketch and that I'm not a particularly good artist anyway, he was able to participate in the session as he normally would. Incidents such as these do provide moments of levity and often give some respite and relief from the rigours and strains that more frequently inhabit Asperger relationships, but even though these two situations are funny, they can still be viewed through a communication 'lens' in that they require some degree of clarification or interpretation.

Whilst this all may sound very useful stuff in that NT spouses now know that the words and behaviour of their AS partners are capable (with or without help) of better understanding through clarification, interpretation or translation, this still leaves them asking, 'But why?' 'What is it about my husband that makes him this way?' Why do we think and react differently to so many things?' It is at this point in counselling that I introduce the clients to the concepts of theory of mind, central coherence theory and executive functioning in an effort to develop for the benefit of both clients, how it is that the AS mind works. It is to these three, fundamentally important cognitive functions that I now want to turn.

Theory of mind

In order for a person to have an adequate theory of mind ability, it requires them to be reasonably competent in considering how things such as situations, circumstances, events and experiences may appear from the perspective of another person. Now it is fair to say that there are many occasions when even the best of us may be under pressure at work, stressed in a relationship or generally feeling tired or under par, and accordingly our ability to use our theory of mind is adversely affected. However, in general terms, people with AS are considered to have poor theory of mind, albeit this will depend upon where any particular individual is on the Asperger spectrum. The higher up the Asperger spectrum the individual is considered to be then the higher the likelihood that he will have poor theory of mind. First Order theory of mind describes where one person is able (or less able in the case of an AS person) to 'get into' the mind of another person, but there is also an assumption on the part of the AS person that NT people know what they, the AS person, is thinking. By way of some examples, one of my male (AS) clients, Richard, went without his wife to a party being held by his near neighbours, Tony and Jean. He was asked by Tony, 'Where's your wife?' Without any consideration of Tony's feelings, Richard casually responded, 'I thought you knew, my wife doesn't like Jean so she's not coming.' Another of my male (AS) clients would regularly 'disappear' at family functions, weddings or parties. This was interpreted as being very rude by all concerned, but his assertion to his wife (on the basis of him having a poor theory of mind) was, 'I feel uncomfortable with groups of people and I don't like idle chit-chat, I thought you knew that.'

One of my female (NT) clients got very frustrated and eventually upset that her (AS) husband wouldn't share with her any of his daily work experiences. His assertion when challenged by her was, 'You know what I do for work, that's where we met. What else can I tell you?' He assumed on the basis that he had met his wife whilst working for the same company, she would know what his everyday activities entailed. Gisela Slater-Walker explains in *An Asperger Marriage (2002)* that her husband, Chris, had only ever told her once during their 11-year relationship that he loved her; from his perspective, once was enough. His logic presumably being that if he had fallen out of love with her at any time he would have told her! Here, Chris displays a lack of awareness of Gisela's needs for emotional sustenance.

First Order theory of mind then relates to one person seeing things from the perspective of another person, i.e. on any given subject what does person A consider is the perspective of person B? Second Order theory of mind presents a more difficult challenge; what does person A think is the perspective of person B regarding the perspective of person C? If First Order theory of mind is difficult for AS people, Second Order theory of mind is virtually impossible! It is in situations where the person with AS doesn't know or understand the perspective of the other person that the *chameleon effect* that I alluded to in the previous chapter comes into being. It's fair to say that at one time or another we all face situations where we are uncertain of what we are supposed to do and so we copy the actions of others to make ourselves less conspicuous, less self-conscious. The problem with people with AS is that they have to do this most of the time, changing as they do to fit into their new surroundings, imitating and mimicking the people that form their immediate environment. The old adage 'When in Rome do as the Romans do' was never more apt than when it is applied to people with AS.

Central coherence theory

If you ask a person, 'By how many senses do human beings live and survive?' The usual answer is, 'Five: sight, sound, touch, taste and smell.' In reality, however, we live by seven senses (some would say more), the other two being our 'vestibular sense' and our sense of 'proprioception'. Our vestibular sense operates from the vestibular system in our inner ear that is filled with fluid and enables us to balance when we move about. I'm sure that most people have experienced a sense of imbalance at some time, which could be as a result of a viral or bacterial infection of the inner ear or perhaps after spinning quickly whereby the brain receives confused messages.

Using receptors in our muscles and tendons, our sense of proprioception relates to information unconsciously processed in the brain as to how our limbs and muscles are responding to external stimuli. If we didn't have this sense we would have to apply high levels of mentally exhausting, conscious energy to all of our physical movements, and we would have difficulty organising and co-ordinating all of our joint and muscle movements at the speed necessary to function properly. As an example, many people with poor proprioception are unable to perform effectively in sporting activities. Even outside of the realms of sport, poor proprioception can cause people to be clumsy, i.e. the feedback from the receptors in your fingers might lead you to believe you have a firmer grip on a mug or glass than you actually do have, and ultimately the mug or glass is dropped and shatters on the hard floor or spills on the carpet. Sometimes, when people have been bedridden for a time and they then try to get out of bed suddenly, they are uncertain how much pressure to assert with their feet on the floor and they may either stumble and then recover, or collapse in a heap. Quite often, in a 'Herman Munster' type fashion, I open doors with an almighty 'bang' as the door hits the wall…simply because the receptors in my hands and arms are misreading the information as to how much energy I am required to exert at the time.

So how do the senses by which we live and central coherence theory relate to one another? Well, central coherence theory relates to the absorption all of the information received by our brain from all of our senses. The problem is that, whereas NT people are generally able to receive that information in such a way as to be able to filter out what they don't need and still be able to make the remainder meaningful, AS people are less well equipped to do this. Generally speaking, NT people live in a 'world of gist' whereby not all of the incoming information is necessary to be able to give meaning to something, and elements from one situation can be transferred to a similar situation without too much difficulty. Whereas the AS person, who doesn't have the filtering system necessary to remove any extraneous information, lives in a 'world of infinite detail' and has great difficulty determining what is meaningful and what isn't from the plethora of information their brain is receiving. An exceptionally good advert published in the *Guardian Weekend* magazine (15 May 2004) by the National Autistic Society read:

> When a person with autism [Asperger Syndrome] walks into a room the first thing they see is: a pillow with a coffee stain shaped like Africa, a train ticket sticking out of a magazine, 25 floorboards, a remote control, a paperclip on the mantelpiece, a marble under the chair, a crack in the ceiling, 12 grapes in a bowl, a piece of gum, a book of stamps sticking out from behind a silver picture frame... So it's not surprising they ignore you completely. People with autism [Asperger Syndrome] tend to see too much detail in everything, so they can't always tell what's important. (my wording in brackets)

I'm reminded of some clients of mine who like to dine out regularly, their favourite food being Italian. Whilst the local Italian restaurant offered fine cuisine and they had dined there regularly to the satisfaction of them both, it was her desire to try a different restaurant. From her perspective (world of gist), one Italian restaurant is pretty much like another and accordingly, going somewhere different shouldn't have presented any problems. However, from his perspective (world of infinite detail), he was quite severely challenged by the prospect. He wanted to know exactly how far away the 'new' restaurant was, what time would they get there and how long would it take, was the car park nearby and was it secure, how big was the restaurant in comparison to their usual one, where would they be sitting, how many other people would be there and would he know anyone, were the tables suitably spaced out or were they close together, was there background music, what sort of people went there?... and much more! It became such a chore to consider going somewhere else that they continued going to their usual place, much to her annoyance and his relief!

Having poor central coherence can render the AS person having to work much harder than the NT person just to do the same thing: to take in information and act upon it. How unfair would it be to expect a student to do twice the amount of homework just to obtain the same marks, or for a graduate to have to take twice as many exams to achieve the same qualification? Homework and exams, however, can be put to one side or forgotten about, even if only temporarily; having poor central coherence is with you permanently. It never leaves you, it goes with you wherever you go and affects everything you do!

Executive functioning

Executive functioning is said to be the means by which our brain interprets all of the information received from our senses and then uses it to perform cognitive functions such as planning things, abstract thinking, employing our working memory, creating mental representations, applying socially acceptable conventions whilst at the same time censoring inappropriate practices and, ultimately, decision making. Imagine then, on the one hand being in possession of a mass of information, sifting out what you considered was superfluous, analysing what was left, developing thoughts around how this remaining information might be used or if it was necessary to gain more, and then being able to make a decision, be it business, educational, political or social, based on all of this mental engineering.

On the other hand, imagine if your ability to use your theory of mind was inadequate; you were uncertain of what people around you were thinking, what they wanted or needed; imagine if you were totally confounded by the sheer volume of sensory information loading into your brain at any one time and your weak central coherence didn't permit you to dump what you didn't need. How confident would you be that any subsequent decision you took was the right one?

Quite clearly, we rely on our theory of mind and central coherence abilities to feed into the executive system of our brain (Figure 4.5) in order that we can carry out the cognitive functions necessary to engage with other people and our environments. Poor theory of mind and weak central coherence negatively impact upon our ability to engage this way. The problem is that most AS people don't know this. They assume, until they are told otherwise, that they are functioning perfectly normally and that everyone else thinks and feels the same way as they do!

Processing time

I want to mention briefly 'processing time' as this is another much misunderstood aspect of communication between an AS person and their NT

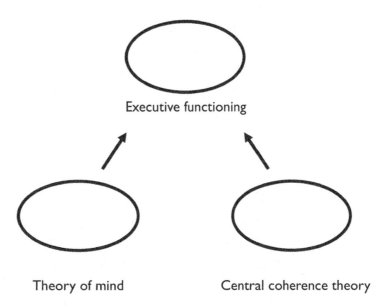

Figure 4.5

partner. On average, when an AS person is spoken to, it takes them eight seconds to process what has been said to them and to respond appropriately (note this is the average time, so some people will take even longer). If you are an NT partner in a relationship with an AS man, you may already have experienced this, but maybe you didn't realise what was happening. Very often an NT spouse will ask a question of her AS partner, and whilst he is processing the information she will assume he is unable or unwilling to provide a suitable reply and say something like, 'There you are, you can't answer me can you, well can you? No! This happens all the time with you!' In reality what this does is to add further information to that which he is already trying to process and thereby makes his response time even longer, whilst at the same time she becomes ever more frustrated or angry. As an alternative to not providing an answer at all during the processing time, the AS partner may try to gain more time by repeating back to her what she has just said to him, e.g. (NT partner) 'Why didn't you tell me about this before?' (AS partner) 'Why didn't I tell you about this before?' or may try to divert the question by taking the conversation off at a tangent, such as, 'Before we discuss that, what's going on with the plumber, you told me you were sorting that?' In both cases, with either the echoed response or the attempted divert, he is trying to gain valuable time by which he can process the original question. If you have any doubt as to the effect of an eight-second response time where a reply is not forthcoming, try it! Wait until a friend or colleague asks you something and then, before answering, count eight seconds in your mind and then answer. Don't be surprised if you get some very strange responses!

I've known many NT spouses who had thought for years that their AS husband or partner had been purposefully trying to annoy them or wind them up by employing a tactic of not answering when spoken to, repeating the question back to them or diverting to a different subject. However, by using such a simple tactic as to allow for processing time to occur, many arguments and misunderstandings in AS–NT relationships can be avoided.

Cassandra phenomenon

I want to conclude this chapter by giving some recognition to a debilitating condition that can be experienced by the spouses of people with AS (often at the hands of family members, friends and colleagues), that is referred to as the Cassandra phenomenon. I think the following quote from the Families of Adults Affected by Asperger Syndrome (FAAAS) website (www.faas.org/doc.php?40) aptly explains the naming of this syndrome.

> I ended up feeling that no one would listen to me and came up with a name for the 'syndrome' that affects the non-AS spouse: The CASSANDRA PHENOMENON, Cassandra being the Greek mythological character who was given the gift of prophecy, but also the curse of having no one believe her even though she was right! (Anonymous, Massachusetts, 1999)

It is usually both a blessing and a relief when an NT spouse learns about AS (perhaps from a magazine article or a TV programme) and feels she now has an explanation for her husband's unusual behaviour. But it is demoralising and extremely frustrating if the AS husband rejects her theory out of hand. Imagine then, as a next step the NT spouse seeks support from the extended family; 'Perhaps mum-in-law might be able to give me some childhood history of my husband?' She optimistically thinks this might help, only to be told quite firmly, 'There's nothing wrong with my son, I suggest you look a bit closer to home!' Not only have the NT spouse's hopes been dashed with regard to gaining support from her mother-in-law, but the relationship between herself and all of her in-laws has probably now been seriously damaged and even more tension may be generated at home between her and her husband.

Still intent on gaining credibility for the theory that her husband exhibits Asperger-type behaviour, she then seeks the support of people in her and her husband's social network. The problem here might be that the AS husband (assuming the wife's theory is indeed correct), is one of those 'chameleon-like' people that can fit in reasonably well in certain social situations. A typical type of response in these circumstances from the NT spouse's friend might then be, 'I think he's a little different to other men, but I think that's kind of cute. I don't think he's as bad as you are making out.' Ironically, it may have been the 'cute difference' that initially attracted the NT partner to her AS spouse when they first met!

No way forward here then for our NT partner as people outside the relationship only see a limited part of the AS man. They don't experience him in an emotional context, they don't witness his rituals, his routines or his inflexible lifestyle that occur for the most part within the confines of the home. FAAAS gave further credence to this problem in 1977 when they described it thus:

> FAAAS came up with the term 'Mirror Syndrome' to explain the way NT spouses and NT family members are adversely affected by AS behaviours, especially undiagnosed AS in adults. NT family members, over time, begin to reflect the persona of AS behaviours we live with, twenty-four seven. We are isolated, no one validates us, we lose friends and family, and we feel like 'hostages' in our own homes. (FAAAS website)

My reasons for drawing attention to this condition, be it termed Cassandra phenomenon or Mirror Syndrome, is to let NT partners who are in this plight know that their situation is recognised. It is known that loneliness, anxiety and depression can result when they try to tell people about their AS situation, but they are not listened to or are thought of as being melodramatic or even paranoid. I also hope that family members, friends and colleagues may in future take notice and be more prepared to hear what 'Cassandra' has to say.

Chapter 5

Stage Five: Visual Aids for Understanding: What the Counsellor Does

Your pain is the breaking of the shell that encloses your understanding.

Kahlil Gibran

The emphasis of the Asperger therapy that I undertake is on building each new stage of my model on the one that precedes it. Just as the first floor of a multi-storey building should be placed on a firm foundation before the higher levels are then built on top of each other, so each stage of my model has to be in place before the next one can be developed.

If we briefly visit the model thus far we can see that Stage One is about gaining an initial knowledge of what AS is about and identifying that it is experienced differently, but nonetheless very profoundly by both AS and NT partners. Stage Two looks at the relationship between AS and NT partners from an individual perspective in order that their personal slant on the relationship can be considered. In continuing with the building metaphor, each partner has the opportunity to be a designer in what the future relationship (assuming there's going to be one) might look like. This stage also provides for each partner (designer) to get to know the counsellor (engineer) better on a one-to-one basis.

Stage Three is the start of co-counselling and where a higher level of knowledge about AS is developed through reading and film material. From this material the partners are invited to try to identify what some of the AS induced relationship problems are that they experience. Stage Four raises the level of knowledge again and starts to identify how it is that each partner functions differently from a neurological perspective, and why it is they have differing perspectives on things. Indeed, when some of the neurological explanations are given, one would be more surprised if AS and NT people did see things the same way! In this chapter I want to take things one step further and explain how I take the theoretical themes from the last chapter and apply visual ways of illustrating them so they can more easily be clarified, interpreted or translated. People with AS usually find that visual explanations of things such as drawings or diagrams are much easier to understand, as are things that are written down.

Fairly early on in this stage I regularly ask my clients to do a priorities exercise for me in the counselling room. Armed with paper and pen, I ask them to write down what is at the forefront of their respective minds at this present time; what (if any) are the issues that are giving them cause for concern at some level or may even be having a really serious negative impact on their lives. I suggest they write about five things each. Now given that the clients are attending my counselling/therapy sessions because of the problems in their relationship, one would imagine that mention of this would appear on each partner's list, probably at the top of the list or certainly near to it.

However, Figures 5.1 and 5.2 are the lists produced by two of my clients who did this exercise and are fairly typical of what happens. Figure 5.1 is the NT partner's list and Figure 5.2 the AS partner's list and, as can be seen, the NT partner has placed their relationship at the top of her list as priority number one, but the AS partner has placed their relationship at number four on his list. From the NT partner's perspective this would probably be the response she expected from her 'unfeeling' AS spouse! However, I then explain that this is not a statement on his part that he doesn't care about her or that he doesn't think their relationship is impor-tant, rather an example of central coherence theory at work. She as an NT person living in the world of gist, can either filter out everything else trou-bling her, or at least prioritise things in the order that they affect her, hence the relationship problem is placed top of her list. He on the other hand, as an AS person living in a world of infinite detail, is being bombarded with

<table>
<tr><td>

<u>Jane (NT Partner)</u>

1. Our relationship
2. Problems at work
3. Debts
4. Parents not in very good health (old age)
5. Losing friends because of the Asperger Syndrome

</td><td>

<u>*John (AS Partner)*</u>

1. *Must try to get some overtime to pay debts*
2. *Don't like my boss*
3. *Have to get car MOT'd*
4. *Must try not to upset my wife*
5. *Finish DIY jobs*

</td></tr>
</table>

Figure 5.1   **Figure 5.2**

masses of information that he cannot filter and so he will respond to this exercise in terms of whatever is most troubling for him at that time. Hence he placed some of his issues 'before' the relationship in terms of what was affecting him then and there, but not 'above' the relationship in terms of how he feels about his spouse. Exercises like this, whilst initially appearing to confirm the NT partner's thoughts about lack of care and concern, actually serve to help NT people to understand some of the problems that AS people experience.

From a theory of mind perspective, the male client may have little understanding of how his prioritising will have the potential (as it did in this case) to upset his wife. It may be appropriate at this time to reiterate the maxim previously presented to the clients: 'I may not understand your feelings, but I acknowledge and respect them.'

Another visual method I use in the counselling room demonstrates how focusing on other issues can overwhelm the relationship. I take a blank piece of A4 paper and draw upon it a square representing the couple's relationship; Panel A of Figure 5.3 represents just such a relationship (Jane and John). I then write on a second piece of paper the items my AS client listed in the priorities exercise and include a further item that loosely covers 'other matters', and I either cut or tear these into smaller pieces of paper (as per Panel B) and then overlay them on the first piece of paper (see Panel C). In a very graphic way it can be seen that there is not much left of the relationship apparent because all of the other items are getting in the way! This exercise is provided in Handouts 5.1 and 5.2 at the end of this chapter and can be done in the session by the clients under the direction of the counsellor.

Very often, the NT partner isn't even aware of the issues that may be confronting her AS spouse. She may have tried to make herself aware when asking him, 'What's wrong, is there something on your mind?' only to be greeted with a negative response suggesting that there isn't. By opening up these issues of central coherence theory and theory of mind in the counselling room, any sense of exclusion, embarrassment or of being criticised (on the part of both partners) can be overcome and issues that are especially challenging to the AS partner can be shared and dealt with as a couple. If coping with all of this unfiltered sensory information is so mentally challenging to the AS partner, it must also be mentally exhausting, and indeed it is!

I recall one day going to the kitchen area at Relate to make myself a cup of tea. On entering the room I couldn't see two feet in front of me because of the steam emanating in vast quantities from the hot water urn. It was quite an old-style urn and the water level had been allowed to get too low whilst the heating system was still turned up high. I immediately turned the heating level to low and when the steam cleared, I then topped up the water. It was whilst I was having the cup of tea that I subsequently made

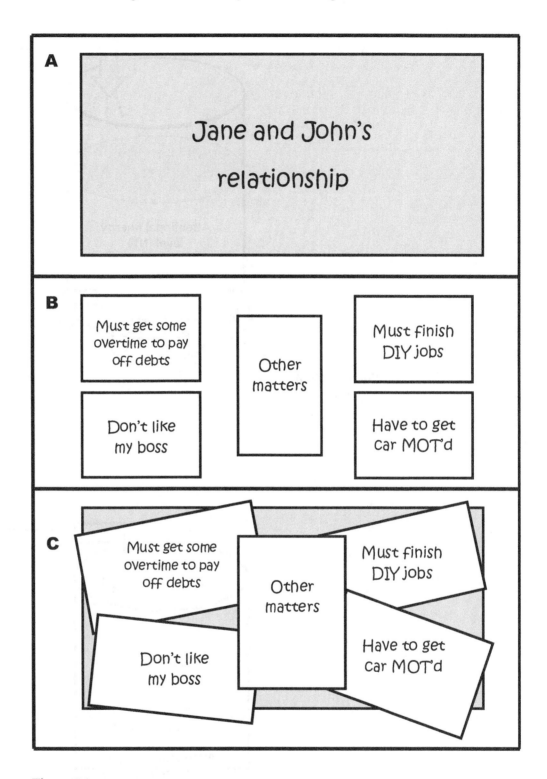

Figure 5.3

that I started to think about the analogies between the urn and the situations that occur for some people who have lots of things to do, but not sufficient energy to do them. In applying this train of thought to mental energy, I came up with the *Attentional Energy Model* (see Figure 5.4).

If we think of the urn as being the human mind and having a capacity to hold sufficient attentional energy to apply to our cognitive functions, then

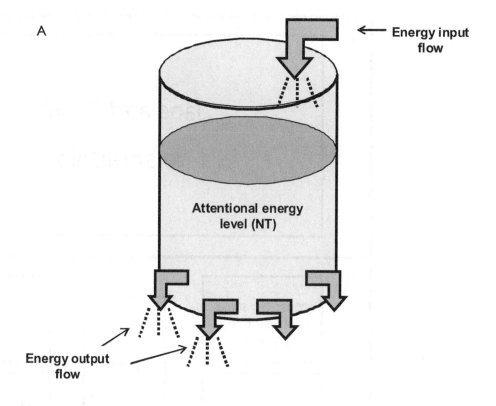

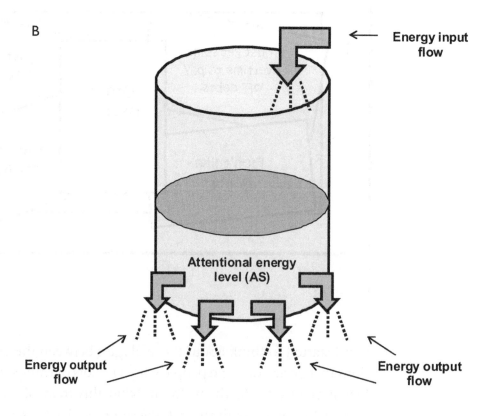

Figure 5.4: Attentional energy model *cont.*

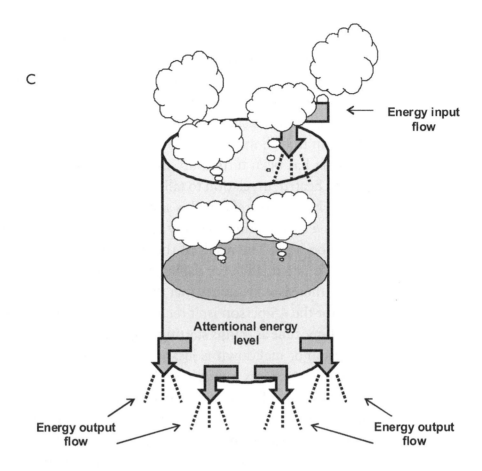

Figure 5.4: Attentional energy model *cont.*

in order to carry out our everyday activities it is paramount that the outflow of this energy doesn't exceed the input. I'm sure we all experience times when we have a lot on our minds and we're feeling tired, but there are things that need to be planned, or we have to remember things or we need to be creative, but we just don't seem to be able to muster enough attentional energy to be able to do these things.

Given what I've already explained about people with AS and executive functioning, I want you to think about Figure 5.4A in terms of sufficient attentional energy flowing into the human mind so as to be able to deal adequately and competently with one or two cognitive outputs simultaneously (e.g. consider a couple of the items on John's list at Figure 5.2). Indeed, the NT mind would usually filter out the less important items at this time and prioritise the remainder, thereby not opening up too many 'energy output taps' at one time and using too much attentional energy. However, if we look at Figure 5.4B we see that the same amount of energy is coming in, but there are more energy sapping 'taps' turned on (consider trying to deal with all of the items on John's list at the same time). Because the AS mind cannot filter out that which is unnecessary to deal with at that time, the attentional energy level is getting very low and on such occasions is insufficient for the AS person to deal competently with anything.

Indeed, in terms of cognitive functioning, it's fair to say that Figure 5.4A is a fair representation of how the NT mind works most of the time whilst Figure 5.4B is more typical of how the AS mind often works.

In developing this model even further, consider how much more difficult it becomes in using what remaining attentional energy we have left, if we begin to feel, metaphorically speaking, 'hot under the collar', or that 'the heat has been turned up' in any given situation, or that 'things are getting heated' in relation to talking to a spouse or perhaps a supervisor at work. Figure 5.4C reflects this and demonstrates a situation where there is a low level of attentional energy combined with the temperature of the urn being too high. The result of these things happening simultaneously for the urn is potentially very damaging because if action isn't taken to rectify things, there is a possibility that the urn may implode. Likewise, if the situation for the AS person isn't rectified when low attentional energy occurs at the same time as things starting to get 'a bit heated', then a psychological implosion or meltdown is just as likely. When I explained this model to some of my clients, one particular male AS partner said, 'That exactly describes how I feel. It seems to me that NT people can make progress in their daily lives without too much mental energy being used, whereas I have to use loads of mental energy just to remain static.'

If we assume that the lack of attentional energy for the AS partner is directly attributable to struggling with a poor theory of mind and weak central coherence, there are written strategies that can assist the NT partner to reduce stress in these circumstances. These strategies are shown in Figures 5.5 and 5.6. The attentional energy model and the strategy lists are available to be copied as Handouts 5.3, 5.4 and 5.5 at the end of this chapter.

I want to turn now to something called 'transactional analysis'. It sounds complicated, but it actually refers to examining (an analysis of) the way that people communicate (transact) with one another. Apart from this being an interesting subject matter for me in terms of how my AS and NT clients interact with one another, I've found it to be something else that lends itself very well to being explained visually. The essence of transactional analysis is that although we are the person that we are at any particular stage of our life, we have the capacity to act differently at various times depending upon how we feel at that time in relation to other people.

There are three psychological states of mind (referred to as ego-states) that we employ when communicating with other people; these are the 'parent' state, the 'adult' state and the 'child' state. I've found that when explaining these ego-states to my clients it helps to give each one a description. Therefore I explain that the 'parent' ego-state is largely a *prescriptive* role that we can identify with when we see this carried out in an appropriate way by a parent towards their child. Of course, being

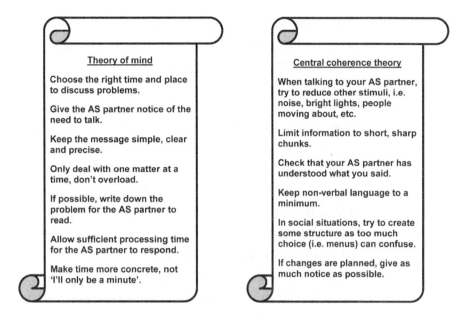

Theory of mind

Choose the right time and place to discuss problems.

Give the AS partner notice of the need to talk.

Keep the message simple, clear and precise.

Only deal with one matter at a time, don't overload.

If possible, write down the problem for the AS partner to read.

Allow sufficient processing time for the AS partner to respond.

Make time more concrete, not 'I'll only be a minute'.

Central coherence theory

When talking to your AS partner, try to reduce other stimuli, i.e. noise, bright lights, people moving about, etc.

Limit information to short, sharp chunks.

Check that your AS partner has understood what you said.

Keep non-verbal language to a minimum.

In social situations, try to create some structure as too much choice (i.e. menus) can confuse.

If changes are planned, give as much notice as possible.

Figure 5.5   Figure 5.6

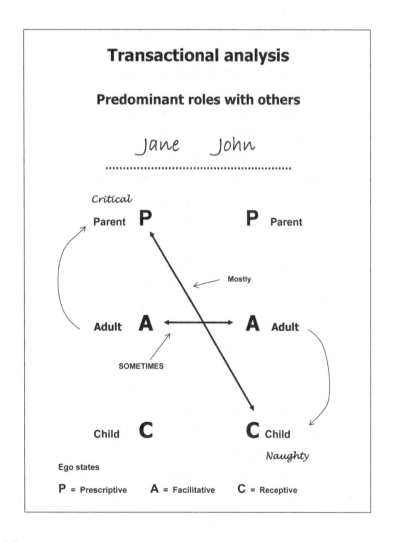

Figure 5.7

excessively prescriptive is not beneficial to either the child or it's relationship to the parent. I describe the 'adult' ego-state as being primarily a *facilitative* one that encourages personal growth and a sense of autonomy in those we relate to. But, of course, if used in excess to the point of total acquiescence and without recourse to some form of occasional sanction, being overly facilitative can have negative repercussions also. The 'child' ego-state is predominantly a *receptive* one where in the normal course of things a child is suitably cared for at an emotional level and receives the necessary guidance in social and life skills to prepare it for life in general. However, if the child perceives that the parent is excessively prescriptive as described above, or if there is a parenting need either in terms of the level of emotion shown to the child or if the parent is absent a lot or unreliable in terms of making promises and not keeping them, then the child may feel detached from the parent and emotionally vulnerable.

It is the relationship between these ego-states that is important and the reader should remember that one doesn't have to be a child to be acting in a 'child' ego-state. Neither does one have to be a grown up to behave in a 'parent' or 'adult' ego-state. If you look at Figure 5.7 you can observe a situation where both Jane and John sometimes function at the 'adult' to 'adult' ego-state. In this healthy relational situation they are able to create a facilitative relationship, but then subject to various influences the balance in the relationship changes.

Jane, for example, may have suddenly felt that John's behaviour was inappropriate or uncaring and she may have challenged him about it and in so doing moves to the 'parent' ego-state. John, believing that Jane is being unfairly critical of him, feels vulnerable (as a child might) and he moves psychologically to the 'child' ego-state. This is the more usual dynamic between them, Jane as the 'critical parent' and John as the 'naughty child'. I have observed in many of my own clients that prior to therapy this is the dynamic at which they most often function with the NT partner as the parent and the AS partner as the child. As the therapy develops, there is very often (I would like to claim always, but I can't) a shift to the 'adult' to 'adult' dynamic. This exercise is in Handout 5.6 at the end of the chapter to be discussed in session between the clients and counsellor.

Once a 'critical parent' to 'naughty child' transaction has been established between partners, it is often the case that it will continue for some time and can be very difficult to stop. Figure 5.8 shows in simple form how the negative spiral of this particular transaction can be self-generating, i.e. the more John feels that Jane is being critical of him the more he will respond as the vulnerable or naughty child. The more he does this, the more critical Jane will be of him. However, awareness, strategies and practice can reverse this spiral into a positive direction where the 'adult' to 'adult' dynamic is the predominant one between the partners.

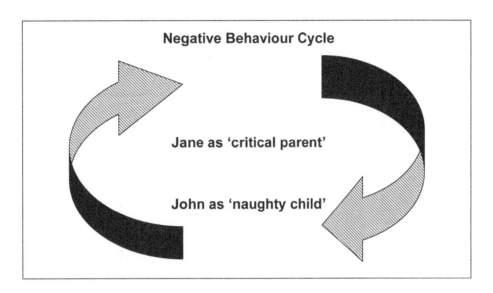

Figure 5.8

A genogram can also be a very good way to illustrate relationships between people in a diagrammatic form and to try to understand how those relationships might have been formed. A genogram is like a family tree and can be used in various ways by counsellors, therapists, etc. For my own part, I explore three aspects of the individual within his or her family or origin to try to understand why that individual is the person they are now; what I refer to as the *person product*. I examine with the clients the 'Relationships' they had with other family members; the 'Rules' within that family system that the individual was expected to comply with and the 'Role' that the individual had in the midst of their parents and/or siblings.

These three 'R's are demonstrated in the genograms I do (see Figure 5.9) by descriptive words and patterned lines. It's right for me say at this point that using genograms with clients doesn't always produce a result, but what can often be observed by the clients in an explicit form is the differences in how each of them was brought up. The AS partner can see before him in graphic form what it was like for his NT wife to be brought up in her family of origin, and be able to compare this with his own experiences as a child and adolescent. Assuming that her upbringing was a good-enough one and that her parents and siblings were good-enough role models, then he can often see what it is she is striving for in her relationship with him and between them and their children, if they have any.

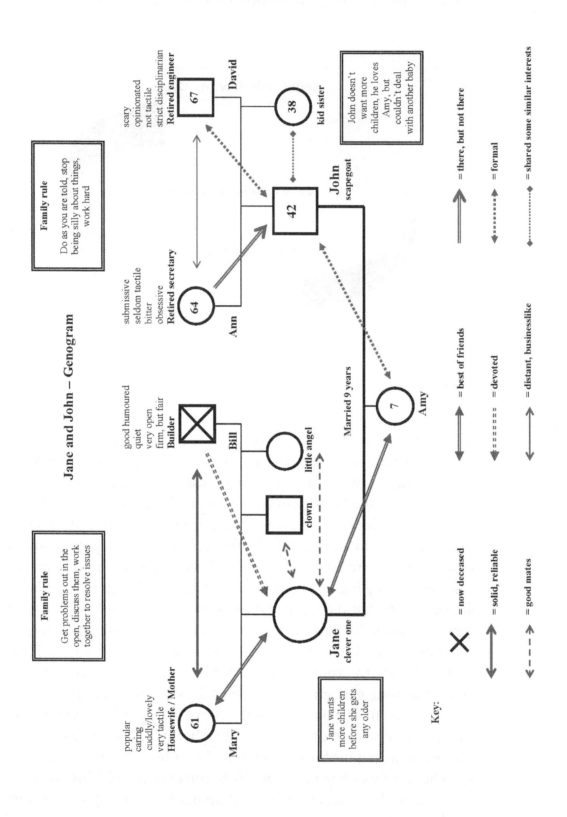

Figure 5.9

In effect, he can learn to model himself on the good role models that are demonstrated in her family of origin.

On first looking at the genogram in Figure 5.9, it looks quite complicated, but these family tree diagrams are built up gradually and sensitively at a pace that is suitable to the clients, as sometimes they can be very revealing and potentially quite upsetting. If we start to pick apart the genogram and look at it in separate chunks, the first thing to explain is that squares represent males and circles represent females. So it can be seen that on the left side of the diagram is Jane, aged 39, her 35-year-old brother and 31-year-old sister, and their mother and father. On the right side there is 42-year-old John, his 38-year-old sister and their mother and father. Jane and John are linked together because they are partners in a relationship. Between the various family members are differently patterned lines that represent a relationship between two specific people. At the foot of the page there is a key that describes what kind of a relationship it is that the lines represents.

The idea of a genogram is to explore and compare the products that the partners have grown to be and the different experiences that each had in their respective original families. I do this by way of the three 'R's that I've already alluded to. If we first of all look at Jane's family of origin, we can see the various words she used to describe her mother; very tactile, cuddly, loving etc. She described her father (now deceased) as firm, but fair, good humoured, very open etc. The principal family rule in Jane's family was that problems should be brought out into the open and resolved by working together as a family. Jane's role in her family was not only that of being the eldest child but, because she was good academically, her parents used to refer to her as the 'clever one'. Her brother was the family 'clown' and her sister was the precious 'little angel'. All of these were roles that the children had and played out to some extent. If we examine the relationship lines between members of Jane's family, we can see that Jane and her mother were the best of friends; her father was devoted to her, and she and her two siblings were good mates. Her mother and father had a relationship she described as solid and reliable. All in all it appears that Jane's family had all the right ingredients for her to have a happy upbringing.

If we now compare this with John's family of origin we can see that John described his mother as being seldom tactile, bitter, obsessive, etc. He described his father as a strict disciplinarian, not tactile at all and even scary. The principal family rule here was to do as you were told, work hard and don't be silly about things. John considered his role in the family to be that of the scapegoat because he seemed to get the blame for everything, even if it was an issue that only involved his parents. He wasn't able to name a role for his younger sister other than his 'kid sister'. The relationship lines in John's family show that his mother was 'there, but not there for him'. I asked him what this meant and he explained that she was present in body, but emotionally and spiritually she wasn't. John's relationship with his dad was quite a formal one, and he couldn't describe a friendship or any emotional ties with his sister, preferring only to say that they shared some similar interests. His parents' relationship was distant and business like. The contrast in John's emotionally austere family to that of Jane's is a stark one.

Another way to view a genogram is at three horizontal, generational levels. It can be seen on Jane's side that her parents' relationship had a positive effect on her and in turn on her relationship with their daughter, Amy. If we compare this with John's side, his parents didn't appear to be happy, which had a detrimental effect on him and subsequently resulted in a very formal relationship between him and Amy, similar to that which existed between him and his father. Another feature of their relationship is that Jane wanted more children before she got too old to have them. John, on the other hand, said that he loved Amy (in his own way), but didn't think he could deal with having another baby.

This particular genogram I created as an amalgam of other genograms that I have done over time. What I don't mean to imply here is that every person who has had a happy childhood will necessarily want to go on and have children of there own, or that an unhappy childhood will render a person as not wanting children. Nor do I imply that every AS child is an unhappy one whereas every NT child is happy. Of course, this is nonsense. However, from an AS perspective, and this is the context in which I am using genograms, the family setting does display a cognitive behavioural setting in which an AS child will learn to do things a certain way, and these ways of being often become ways of life for the AS person unless some form of therapeutic intervention can be made. It is an accepted feature of AS that if a diagnosis is made whilst that person is in their formative years, then there is much more opportunity and potential to change negative views and behaviour into positive ones. If the family setting for a child so diagnosed is a good and happy one, then the social outcomes for the later life of that child are greatly enhanced.

In the work that I undertake with couples, the Asperger diagnosis (where one exists) has usually been made in adulthood. The purpose of using genograms in my therapy, as one intervention amongst many others, is to try to re-model the behaviour of the AS client based on good role models, to encourage each partner to try to appreciate the experiences and perspective of the other, and finally to try to create a new script and a new conjoint form of behaviour for how the couple might live their lives to their mutual advantage. There is a blank genogram form in Handout 5.7 at the end of this chapter to enable the clients to explore with their counsellor the relationships, rules and roles the clients experienced as they grew up in their own families.

One question I am frequently asked by AS–NT couples is 'How can we stop situations developing into arguments that are out of all proportion to the original issue?' They often describe to me arguments that reach 'volcanic' proportions, in that one minute everything appears to be ok, and then something quite innocuous can be said or done that seems to act as a trigger for either a meltdown on the part of the AS partner, or a complete loss of temper on the part of the NT partner. In using the 'volcano' metaphor, I explain to my clients that although the outburst that resulted in the meltdown or temper loss appeared to be sudden and unexpected, the reality is more than likely to be that feelings of anger, frustration, resentment, bitterness, betrayal, low self-esteem, feeling criticised, feeling undervalued and many others, have been bubbling away beneath the surface for some time (just like the molten lava inside a volcano) until the pressure builds up and these feelings cannot be contained any more. It is then that the seemingly innocuous throwaway comment or otherwise irrelevant action becomes the trigger that creates an outlet for the pent-up feelings in all their intensity. As any seismologist will tell you in relation to volcanoes, there will always have been some build up of energy and movement in the earth's crust before a volcano erupted; it doesn't just happen without any warning at all. So it is with emotional outbursts, there are always signs there to be seen, but we seldom act upon them until it's too late!

I acknowledge it is easier said than done, but in answering the question posed by my clients I encourage them to try to read the warning signs and to head off an emotional outburst by combining two particular strategies. Once again, the visual impact of these is significant, the second one particularly so for some clients. The first strategy is called 'The Betari Box' (Figure 5.10). As can be seen from Panel A, the concept is that of 'my attitude' having an impact on 'my behaviour', which is pretty straightforward – I think we would all be surprised if it didn't. However, in turn 'my behaviour' has an impact on 'your attitude', which then affects 'your behaviour'. As can be imagined from this cyclical pattern, it doesn't take very long for a sequence such as this to take place and if all the attitudes and behaviours are negative ones then an argument or a dispute can occur almost before you know it. If you look at Panel B, I have given some ownership of the attitudes and behaviours to my fictitious clients, Jane and John. If we return to our previous scenario involving these partners whereby Jane suddenly felt that John's behaviour changed inappropriately, this is a clear demonstration of her adopting a particular attitude. In turn, Jane's attitude affected her own behaviour and she assumed a critical parent approach towards John. His attitude in response to Jane's behaviour was that he was

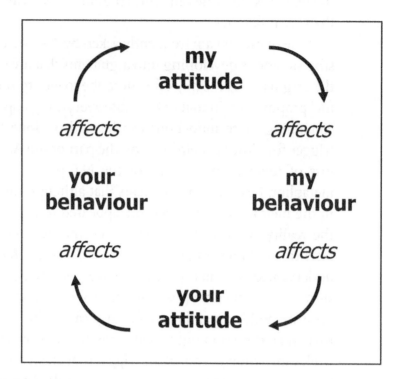

Panel A

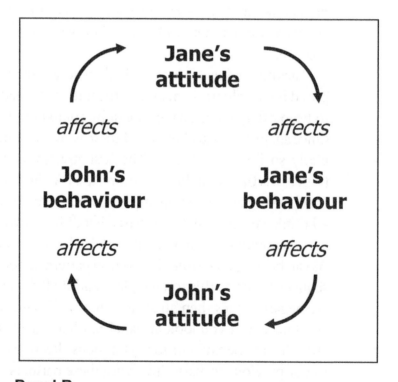

Panel B

Figure 5.10: The Betari Box

being unfairly criticised and so his own resultant behaviour became that of the naughty child.

There is an example of the Betari Box Handout 5.8 at the end of this chapter, which can be copied for the clients to complete Part A with the counsellor and then take away to discuss and complete Part B.

Just because I started this particular cycle of attitude and behaviour with Jane doesn't mean that there is always one partner who is responsible for starting the cycle on its way. It can be much more subtle than that and if negative feelings are rumbling away just beneath the surface on the part of one or both partners, then it is important to get these out into the open in a safe way so that the partners can talk about them. This is where the second strategy comes in.

This strategy, called 'Traffic Light Cards', is based on the three colours of the traffic light signals we see on our roads, namely green, amber and red. We recognise the green light on these traffic signals as meaning we can go ahead; the amber light means we can proceed with caution, whilst the red light means that we stay where we are for now. If we transfer these traffic signal meanings to the emotional situations that can occur in relationships, then by adding a personalised message (or signal) to the relevant coloured card, we can often intervene in a situation that might otherwise go awry. For example, if you look at Figure 5.11 you will see three cards (one could be printed or written on a green card, one on an amber card and the third on a red card). On the green card, suggesting it's ok to go ahead, it reads, 'Let's talk about it now'. On the amber card, suggesting some caution should be applied, it reads, 'Give each other some space, then we'll talk'. The red card suggests there is no progress to be made just yet, and reads, 'We'll agree not to argue now, but set a time to talk about it later'. In each case when using these cards, the message that goes on the cards is peculiar to those particular clients. It's about what works for them! Handout 5.9 at the end of the chapter allows the clients to develop their own 'Traffic Light Cards' and messages.

The reason why the analogy with traffic lights is a good one (I believe and so do many of my clients) is that it caters for various responses to various situations. We all know that drivers wouldn't stop their motor vehicles at a set of green traffic lights if there were no hazards and there was no risk in proceeding. Neither would they just drive straight on and scatter people everywhere if the lights were red and people were crossing the road. Similarly, if you feel there is an issue between you and your partner that needs to be addressed, and you feel it's ok to go ahead, one partner could indicate this intention to the other by placing the green card in an agreed position for the other partner to see and a discussion can ensue. If however, things are a bit more problematic between you and you need to give the issue some degree of thought before you proceed in

Figure 5.11: Traffic Light Cards

discussing it, the amber card could be placed in the pre-arranged position. In both of these ways, by acting proactively and positively to the emotional rumblings going on beneath the surface, the emotional 'volcanic' eruption can often be prevented.

In the worst-case scenario, where the eruption catches one or both partners out, the red card can be used that indicates it is not a good idea to try to proceed at present, but that the issue needs to be discussed when it is safe to do so. I know as I'm writing this that it all sounds very easy, particularly the bit about using the red card. The key words though are practice, practice and more practice. If couples have been experiencing communication problems for 25 years or 5 years, they are unlikely to overcome them by the simple, first-time application of a colour-coded strategy. An acceptance that another perspective exists even if it can't be understood, a willingness to apply strategies (often in tandem) and to practise them, is in my view a cognitive-behavioural approach that presents the best opportunity for resolving communication problems.

In her book *Asperger Syndrome in the Family*, Liane Holliday Willey promotes a particular strategy for people with AS to be able to deal with chaotic or confusing situations. She refers to it as a 'comfort kit' and suggests to people with AS or the parents of AS children that they should carry with them a comfort kit that can contain anything that has a calming effect on that individual. Such items might include ear-plugs to shut out noise, a writing pad to write down their thoughts, concerns or any questions they might want to ask someone later when the confusion has abated, and virtually anything else ranging from bendy toys to squeezy balls and from sticks of bubble gum to a bottle of mineral water. Anything in fact that works for that person: Liane said in her book in relation to comfort kits, 'I think everyone should have one'. I think she's right and so I have taken a leaf out of Liane's book (so to speak) and I recommend to my clients not only her strategy, but also a version of it that I have adopted.

Given that it is usually the male partner who has been diagnosed with AS or at least demonstrates the AS behaviour, and they are less likely to be in a position to carry a 'kit' around with them as a woman might in her handbag or shoulder bag, I have tried to adapt the comfort kit strategy to include things that will fit into a man's wallet or at least be able to be contained within his jacket or trouser pockets. One such thing is a 'comfort card' that is about the same size as a credit card. On this card can be printed a message (Figure 5.12), or a saying (Figure 5.13) or a motto (Figure 5.14) that will act as a comforter to the AS person carrying it when they are anxious, confused or stressed. The message might be from a loved one, the saying might be a proverb or an extract from a poem and the motto might be something agreed between the AS and NT partner or between the AS client and their therapist. If it feels appropriate, the AS partner might have several of these types of cards with them at any one time.

Another thing that fits comfortably into a wallet or a pocket is a photograph. Quite often, if the AS person is upset or anxious, a picture of someone dear to them, be it their wife, mother, daughter or son, can be a very reassuring thing to have in their immediate possession. In addition to this, if one of the comfort cards happens to relate to that particular photograph, e.g. the message on the comfort card from Jane matches her photograph, or the poem about mothers matches a photograph of John's

> *My darling John, through all*
> *your difficult moments, I want*
> *you to remember that I*
> *love you so very much.*
> *Jane*

Figure 5.12

> *Oh lovely name of Mother*
> *that breathes of love and home,*
> *and binds in closest linkship*
> *where'er through life we roam.*

Figure 5.13

> *Yesterday I doubted myself,*
> *today I can achieve.*

Figure 5.14

mother, then both items can work together and be even more reassuring. See the 'Comfort Card Exercise', Handout 5.10 at the end of the chapter.

Another useful item that is a feature of modern technology and can easily be carried in a pocket is an iPod. The blessing of this small but technically brilliant piece of IT is that it can carry a huge amount of information, but more usefully for these purposes it can carry music. For certain people with AS, music can be particularly reassuring when they are feeling under pressure or when things are getting too stressful. As William Congreve wrote in his play 'The Mourning Bride' in 1697, 'Music has charms to sooth a savage breast', and so to remove oneself from the cause of the stress, to switch off to the rest of the world (even for a short duration) and to listen to a favourite piece of music can have a calming effect almost beyond belief. The piece of music might have a special meaning about a particular individual, or it might be significant in terms of the relationship between the AS and NT partners (perhaps the first slow record they danced to), or it can simply be symbolic of a happy time.

Once again, it is possible to link all of these items together so that a comfort card, a photograph and a piece of music all relate to one another, e.g. Jane's message, her photograph and some music that was being played on John and Jane's first date. The important thing is that these things, either individually or combined, have the potential to calm and comfort the AS person when they feel troubled. I'm assured by people with far more technical knowhow than me that all of these things, a comfort card message, a picture of a loved one and a piece of music can be stored in either an iPod or a mobile phone, but for some people the feel of an actual photograph is preferred to one held in a piece of IT equipment.

What I've tried to demonstrate in this chapter, by way of the figures, exercises and handouts, are just a few of the many and various types of visual aids that can be used to help partners in an AS–NT relationship better understand what their relationship is about. They can discover how and why they function together in a negative way and learn how to view things from a positive perspective instead. As I've previously stated, but cannot overstate, visual aids such as genograms, drawings, charts, pictures and lists, etc. impact upon people with AS, so much more than the spoken word. It goes without saying then that if there is a positive impact on the AS partner by the use of visual aids, the knock-on effect is that there is likely to be one for the NT partner also.

When my AS–NT clients talk to me about the problems they have in their relationships, it is apparent that over the course of time they have got themselves into a cycle of negative reinforcement, be it 'critical parent' to 'naughty child' or one partner's negative attitude and behaviour having a direct influence on the other partner's attitude and behaviour. However, through a greater awareness and understanding of Asperger issues, with a commitment to the counselling process and a willingness to practise strategies, it is possible to turn things around so there is a sense of positive reinforcement in the relationship.

Chapter 5: Handouts

Handout 5.1: Priorities Exercise A	Comprises an instruction sheet for the counsellor to follow and use with clients in the session
Handout 5.2: Priorities Exercise B	For the counsellor to photocopy and use in the session in conjunction with Priorities Exercise A
Handout 5.3: Attentional Energy Model	A diagram of the 'Attentional Energy Model' illustrating how levels of mental energy can be appropriately managed (Counsellor to photocopy for clients)
Handout 5.4: Theory of Mind Strategies	A list of 'theory of mind' strategies for the NT partner to improve communication or reduce anxiety in the AS partner (Counsellor to photocopy for clients)
Handout 5.5: Central Coherence Theory Strategies	A list of 'central coherence theory' strategies for the NT partner to improve communication or reduce anxiety in the AS partner (Counsellor to photocopy for clients)
Handout 5.6: Relationship Exercise A	To be photocopied and discussed with the clients, but includes instructions for the clients to complete themselves
Handout 5.7: Relationship Exercise B	To be photocopied and discussed with the clients, but includes instructions for the clients to complete themselves
Handout 5.8: The Betari Box	To be photocopied and discussed with the clients, but includes instructions for the clients to complete themselves
Handout 5.9: Traffic Light Cards	To be photocopied and discussed with the clients, but includes instructions for the clients to complete themselves
Handout 5.10: Comfort Card Exercise	To be photocopied and discussed with the clients, but includes instructions for the clients to complete themselves

Handout 5.1: Priorities Exercise A

Each partner should be asked by the counsellor to write down what is at the forefront of their respective minds at the present time; what are the issues that are giving them cause for concern at some level or may even be having a really serious negative impact on their lives. Suggest they write about five things each.

A discussion should now ensue as to why each client listed the items in the order that they did. Care should be taken to point out that the partners experience the world differently and the AS partner's list will reflect how he cannot filter out superfluous information and will respond to whatever is 'getting at him' at that time.

When the discussion has been had, the items listed by the AS partner should be written by the counsellor onto another piece of paper, each item should then be cut out individually and laid over the relationship square shown in 'Priorities Exercise B'. This gives a very graphic indication of how the AS partner's concerns are getting in the way of the relationship.

Handout 5.2: Priorities Exercise B

The Clients'

Relationship

Handout 5.3: Attentional Energy Model

Diagram A indicates a level of mental energy output that does not exceed the input. This is usually more in keeping with neuro-typical (NT) people who can filter out superfluous sensory information.

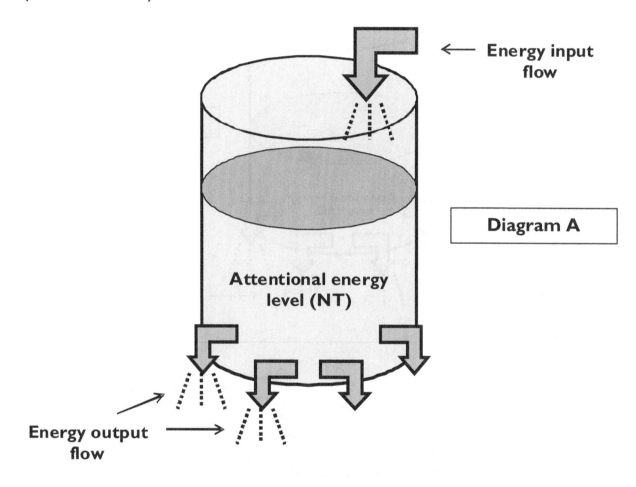

Energy input flow

Diagram A

Attentional energy level (NT)

Energy output flow

Diagram B shows a level of mental energy that is being depleted because there are too many energy 'output' taps open and the output exceeds the input. This is usually more in keeping with Asperger (AS) people who cannot filter out superfluous information.

This situation is further exacerbated in Diagram C when the AS person becomes anxious, frustrated and confused because of their inability to turn off some of the output taps. They are now 'over-heating' and using even more mental energy.

Handout 5.3 *cont.*

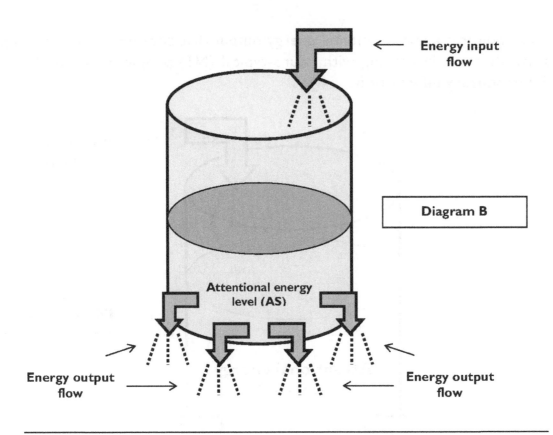

Energy input flow

Diagram B

Attentional energy level (AS)

Energy output flow

Energy output flow

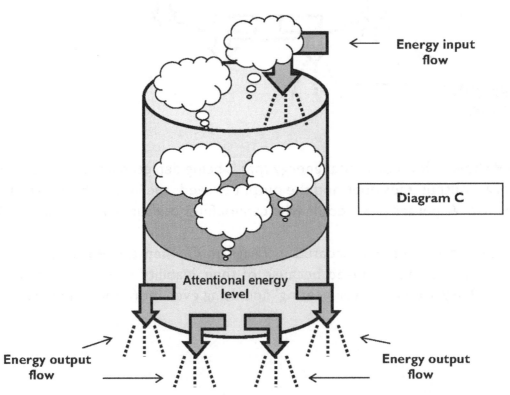

Energy input flow

Diagram C

Attentional energy level

Energy output flow

Energy output flow

Handout 5.4: Theory of Mind Strategies

- Choose the right time and place to discuss problems.

- Give the AS partner notice of the need to talk.

- Keep the message simple, clear and precise.

- Only deal with one matter at a time, don't overload.

- If possible, write down the problem for the AS partner to read.

- Allow sufficient processing time for the AS partner to respond.

- Make time more concrete, not 'I'll only be a minute'.

Handout 5.5: Central Coherence Theory Strategies

- When talking to your AS partner, try to reduce other stimuli, i.e. noise, bright lights, people moving about, etc.

- Limit information to short, sharp chunks.

- Check that your AS partner has understood what you said.

- Keep non-verbal language to a minimum.

- In social situations, try to create some structure as too much choice (i.e. menus) can confuse.

- If changes are planned, give as much notice as possible.

Handout 5.6: Relationship Exercise A

Transactional analysis

Predominant roles with others

For couples to get on well together, the predominant relationship between them should be the 'adult' to 'adult' one.

However, sometimes one of you might feel vulnerable or needy (the 'child' ego-state) and induce the other one to provide support or direction (the 'parent' ego-state). This can benefit the relationship provided it doesn't occur all or most of the time.

Or one of you might feel the other has acted irresponsibly and you adopt a 'critical parent' role and thereby induce the other to feel like a 'naughty child'. This will not benefit the relationship at any time.

Work together to see if you can agree what roles each of you adopts that negatively affect your relationship. Each write your name in one of the spaces provided, and using the PARENT, ADULT and CHILD positions under your names, draw lines to link these positions with those under your partner's name to establish a relationship.

If it helps to describe the relationship from your perspective, add descriptive words like 'Vulnerable' or 'Critical' to the words PARENT, ADULT or CHILD.

....

Partner's name   Partner's name

Parent **P**   **P** Parent

Adult **A**   **A** Adult

Child **C**   **C** Child

Handout 5.7: Relationship Exercise B

For this exercise, you should work together as a couple to discuss the RELATIONSHIPS, RULES and ROLES that existed within your own families as you were each growing up. Write your names in the spaces provided next to the grey circle (female partner) and the grey square (male partner). You can then develop the 'family tree' on your side of the graph by using these simple rules:

- FAMILY MEMBERS: To show other family members, draw more circles (females) or squares (males) and write their names next to them.

- RELATIONSHIPS: Draw different coloured or patterned lines between your family members to represent the 'feel' of *that* relationship, then use the key below to describe the relationship, i.e. formal, unhappy, devoted, etc. (see examples).

- ROLES: Write in the roles that you and your family members had, i.e. *the clown, the clever one, the scapegoat*, etc.

- RULES: If necessary, use a blank piece of paper to write down your family rules, i.e. 'let's talk about it' or 'shut up and do as you are told'.

- When you have done this you can discuss any impact your families of origin may have had on your relationship with one another now.

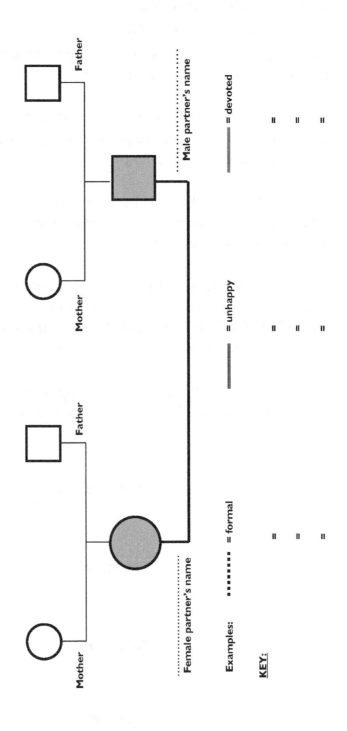

Female partner's name

Male partner's name

Examples: ••••••• = formal   ══════ = unhappy   ═══ = devoted

    ═   ═   ═

    ═   ═   ═

KEY:

Handout 5.8: The Betari Box

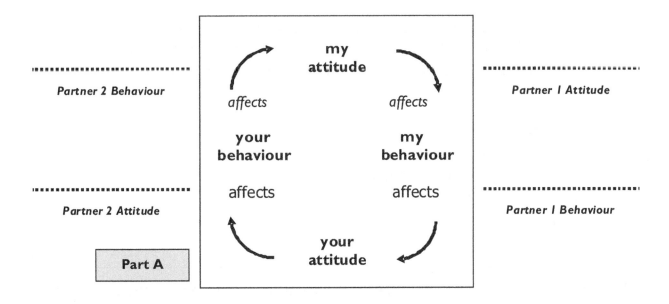

The counsellor, using Part A, should write an example of an attitude on the 'Partner 1 Attitude' line and ask the clients to offer an example of that same (fictitious) person's behaviour on the 'Partner 1 Behaviour' line. They should then be invited to give an example of what attitude this may produce on the 'Partner 2 Attitude' line and what behaviour may result on the 'Partner 2 Behaviour' line. They clients can now complete Part B by inserting their own names on the dotted lines and taking the handout away to discuss and complete in the same way regarding a recent argument they had.

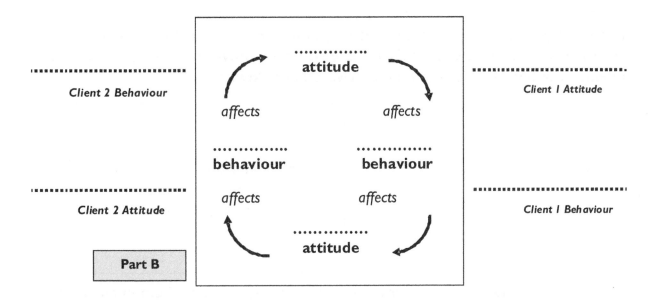

Handout 5.9: Traffic Light Cards

The counsellor should ask the clients if they think some arguments between them could be talked about at the time without exacerbating them. If so, what message might they give each other on the first card to indicate they can 'Go ahead'?

> Consider using black ink on
> a green card or green ink
> on a white card?

If an argument cannot be immediately resolved, what message might the clients give each other to indicate this, but also their willingness to 'Proceed with caution' later?

> Consider using black ink on
> an amber card or amber/orange ink
> on a white card

If there is potential for the argument to continue or worsen if the clients try to resolve it immediately, what useful message can they convey to each other to 'Stop' talking now, but resume when things have calmed down?

> Consider using black ink on
> a red card or red ink on a
> white card?

The clients should also agree how to use the cards, i.e. place them in an agreed position on the dining room table or the kitchen work surface for both to see.

Handout 5.10: Comfort Card Exercise

Comfort cards are designed for people with AS to carry with them for reassurance when they are feeling anxious, agitated or confused. Here is an example of one that Jane wrote for her husband John:

My darling John, through all
your difficult moments, I want
you to remember that I
love you so very much.
Jane

Work together to see what can be put onto 'comfort cards' to help the AS partner to relax through times of stress (if you both have AS your counsellor will help you). The 'cards' below can be used to practise this skill.

Now consider and discuss what other forms of 'comfort' are available to you, e.g. a photograph of your partner or a parent; a favourite song or tune saved on a mobile phone or iPod.

Chapter 6

Stage Six: Developing Strategies: What the Clients Do

A little knowledge that acts is worth infinitely
more than much knowledge that is idle.

Kahlil Gibran

In every case of couple counselling where AS is a presenting problem, serious and careful consideration has to be given to the specific issues that create difficulties for *that* couple in order that appropriate strategies can be devised to overcome those difficulties. Indeed, of all the couples that I've seen for Asperger counselling, the main similarity is that in the vast majority of cases it is the male partner who has AS. In every other respect the couples are different in either the problems they experience or the degree to which they experience them.

I can say with certainty that to date I have not dealt with any two Asperger couples where the difficulties of communication, socialisation and imaginative thinking, or the degree to which certain traits are displayed, have been exactly the same.

It is because couples present so differently and uniquely with their Asperger problems that the preceding stages of my counselling model are all extremely important in determining what those problems are and what might be considered to help the clients overcome them. Each of the couples that form the case studies in this book has been carefully taken through this process in order to have their own idiosyncratic needs met.

In some cases I have been instrumental in designing strategies for my clients; on other occasions I have borrowed or adapted some from the numerous counselling books already in existence. What is crucially important though, is whether a particular strategy is suitable to the needs of *that* couple. Where the clients can be encouraged to devise and own the strategies themselves, this can be much more advantageous in terms of the couple working together to think about the types of strategies they will use, and then working together to try to make them succeed. It should also be remembered that any strategy, be it a list, a written instruction, a chart or any form of exercise can be fine-tuned so as to obtain the desired effect. Sometimes it is a case of trial and error, but if a strategy has the feel of 'too much too soon' or it's not having sufficient effect, then fine-tuning and continued practice really can make a difference.

Sometimes a strategy can take the form of a very brief social story (see *My Social Stories Book*, Gray and White 2002), where problem scenarios, upsetting family situations or social encounters may require that precise written instructions are followed to prevent such events happening again or to resolve one if it has already happened. Ordinarily, social stories are used with children with autistic spectrum disorders, but they can also be very effective when used in an adult version. From a cognitive-behavioural perspective, once the story or the form of words becomes second nature (to the AS partner in particular) and the new behaviour becomes the norm, the written instructions can be made redundant. It is also entirely appropriate to take a strategy designed for one couple and adjust it to the needs of another couple if necessary.

I want now to return to our four case studies so we can see just how certain strategies were used; where the clients may have experienced difficulties with some of them as well as success; how such strategies will have been fine-tuned or changed considerably to better suit the needs of the clients and what some of the outcomes of this form of therapy were. The way that the various stages of the counselling model can be juxtaposed will also be demonstrated.

It is appropriate to remind the reader at this time that the names of the clients used as case studies have been changed as have their circumstances, and pseudonyms used to ensure confidentiality is maintained. However, the relationship issues described in the case studies are real.

Case study 1 – Anne and Bob

With each of the couples featured in the case studies, their presenting problems and how their lives were adversely affected by them can be recalled by briefly revisiting Chapter 2. With regard to Anne and Bob, Anne felt that because of Bob's Asperger behaviour (he had been formally diagnosed), their relationship was affected in the following ways:

- Bob had withdrawn from being intimate with her – he seemed reluctant to kiss or even cuddle Anne.

- Anne felt excluded by Bob because he didn't share his feelings or thoughts with her and seemed unable or unwilling to explain his anger and frustrations to her.

- Talking had become stilted between them; Anne felt it was one-sided (from her) and that Bob didn't respond unless prompted.

- Because of all of the above, Anne felt unsupported in their marriage and more and more isolated from Bob.

Initially, it may be considered wise to try relatively simple strategies to address problems, albeit no strategy or task should ever be complicated. In addressing the first of Anne's concerns as listed above (none of which Bob disagreed with), it was accepted by Bob that when he got home from work every evening, he was usually very tired and often thinking about things that had occurred at work that day. Such things wouldn't normally challenge the NT mind, but from Bob's perspective these things were pre-occupying him to the point that he was mentally drained. In effect they were over occupying his mind and using what little attentional energy reserves he had left. Accordingly, he forgot more often than not to greet Anne with a cuddle or a kiss when he went indoors.

Strategy 1

It was agreed between the clients that a note would be displayed in such a position that when Bob came home from work, he couldn't fail to see it. The note read simply 'Give Anne a kiss and a hug'. Seeing this note would hopefully spur Bob into complying with it. There was some initial trepidation from Bob in that he didn't want the note to be in a conspicuous place where family members or visitors could see it. Anne perfectly well understood this and so the note was placed in the cupboard used as a cloakroom, where Bob hung his jacket every day after work.

Strategy 2

Whilst strategy one was being practised, it was agreed that Bob should try to express his anger, annoyance or frustrations in the best manner open to him, but in a way that was completely safe for both partners. If he wasn't able initially to talk to Anne about things directly, could he at least externalise them in some way with a view to being able to talk about them later? Bob thought that writing down his thoughts and feelings about the key issues that troubled him might be useful and possibly make him feel better. To help him with this, an 'Anger Scratchpad' was devised on which he could write simple scribbled notes about a particular issue or issues that were monopolising his thoughts (see Handout 6.1 at the end of this chapter). As can be seen from Bob's 'Scratchpad' in Figure 6.1, it accommodates those issues that had the most effect on Bob's life, but also accommodates 'other matters' when appropriate. As a further means of helping Bob to understand his own feelings and then share them with Anne, a third strategy was used.

Anger Scratchpad

Me	Anne
Home	Work
Family	Neighbours
Other matters	Other matters

Figure 6.1

Strategy 3

This next strategy is one that I give to the clients and is known as 'What Colour Are You Feeling?' (see Handout 6.2 at the end of this chapter). As with any of my clients who have used this task, Bob took it home and used it in two ways: first he changed the moods on the left-hand side of the document to ones that he could best relate to, and then he named a colour in the corresponding box on the right-hand side against those moods he felt he experienced most regularly, but wasn't always able to explain why (see Figure 6.2).

When clients are invited to do this task the moods and the colours have the potential to be as individual as the client themselves. When I asked Bob, for instance, why the mood 'happy' was represented by the colour blue, he said, 'When I wake up in the morning and look out of my bedroom window, the colour of the sky sets my mood for the day. If it's light blue, I know it's going to be a happy day.' He went on to say, 'Orange for me is neither one colour nor the other (being red and yellow combined), and that's why I think it's sad – because of my AS I sometimes feel that I'm not one thing or the other.'

The second part of this strategy as far as Bob was concerned was for me to create a number of coloured cards that matched each of the colours on the document. These cards were printed and laminated (they could simply be crayoned, painted or printed from a computer) and the arrangement between Anne and Bob was that anytime he felt that one of the moods was affecting him, but couldn't necessarily explain why he was feeling it, he would leave the matching coloured card in an agreed place for Anne to see. The first outcome of this agreed action was that Anne felt 'included' as opposed to pushed away. Furthermore, it gave her the opportunity to undertake the next agreed part of the strategy in that she could gently ask him questions around the mood he was feeling and so develop communication and a sense of sharing between them.

A review of the strategies so far

It seemed apparent that two things were happening with the first of the strategies that Bob had agreed to try. First, on seeing the note when returning home from work, Bob would go to Anne and put his hand on her arm or shoulder and give her a peck on the cheek. Anne later commented on this and stated, 'It's better than nothing, but it's still very formal and not very loving.' The second aspect was what was happening in Bob's mind. He said, 'It feels unnatural to have to kiss and hug Anne because I have a sign reminding me to; I would prefer to just be able to do it naturally.'

Strategy 2 was altogether more enabling for Bob, at least with regard to writing about the things that were troubling him. The immediate effect of

What Colour Are You Feeling?

Name: Bob

Happy

| Blue |

Sad

| Orange |

Anxious

| |

Excited

| |

Depressed

| Black |

Confident

| |

Worried

| Red |

Secure

| |

Insecure

| |

Positive

| Green |

Angry

| Purple |

Tearful

| |

Uncertain

| |

Figure 6.2

this was that he had externalised the issues (if only onto paper) and felt less tense as a consequence; this alone had a positive impact on their relationship. The second aspect of this strategy, if he felt he could, was to talk about these issues with Anne. On one such occasion he wrote on his 'Anger Scratchpad' his feelings about his relationship with his siblings and then shared these feelings with Anne, who had not previously known how he had felt. However, Bob wasn't always able to fulfil the second part of this strategy.

Bob took Strategy 3 on board because, he said, 'I like the idea of colours representing my feelings, it makes sense to me.' As mentioned, Bob adjusted the moods and colours on the 'What Colour Are You Feeling' document so they were relevant to him, and he started placing the appropriate coloured 'mood' cards in the agreed place for Anne to see. Whilst this gave Anne the option to enquire further into his feelings if she so wished, on those occasions that she did, Bob wasn't always able to respond as Anne might have hoped.

What is important to remember here is that strategies in whatever form they take, are not going to change an AS person's behaviour overnight, particularly so if that behaviour has been in place for many years. What seemed to be happening with Anne and Bob was that he could engage in all three strategies to an extent, and certainly showed willing in this respect, but still had some difficulty in taking this further and engaging with Anne at a more meaningful level. Anne was pleased at the changes that Bob had made, but was frustrated that they hadn't progressed further. It was agreed that Bob would see me for a couple of sessions on his own as they both had in Stage Two of my counselling model.

Bob attended alone for the next two sessions, during which time he explained to me, in a very moving and descriptive way, why he struggled to talk to Anne in the very way he was now talking to me! He said, 'When I was courting Anne it was like walking along a straight road; everything was easy to see and I knew where I was going. After we married it was as if we came to a set of crossroads and I couldn't see ahead of me anymore. I still don't know which way to go.' He went on to say, 'A lot has happened since me and Anne married and it's been like a series of explosions, one after the other. I still feel shell-shocked and confused.' In a similarly descriptive way, Bob said, 'When I'm talking to you about Anne or to the people at work about everyday things, it feels safe and I feel relaxed, but sometimes when I'm talking to Anne it feels like I'm walking out onto a frozen pond, and the further I go the riskier it gets.'

When counselling resumed with both clients, Anne was initially hurt to think that Bob could talk to me in such a way, but not to her. She did realise, however, that there was no emotional 'risk' in mine and Bob's communications, but there was in theirs. That said, both to mine and Anne's surprise and delight, Bob said to Anne, 'I think of our marriage as a jigsaw, but with several bits missing and I can't just work out what those bits are'. Enter Strategy 4.

Strategy 4

I conceived this next strategy as a direct result of Bob's last comment. The beauty of it was that I presented both clients with a blank 'jigsaw' puzzle (Handout 6.3) that they could take home and complete in a way that each felt represented what a relationship between partners should look like.

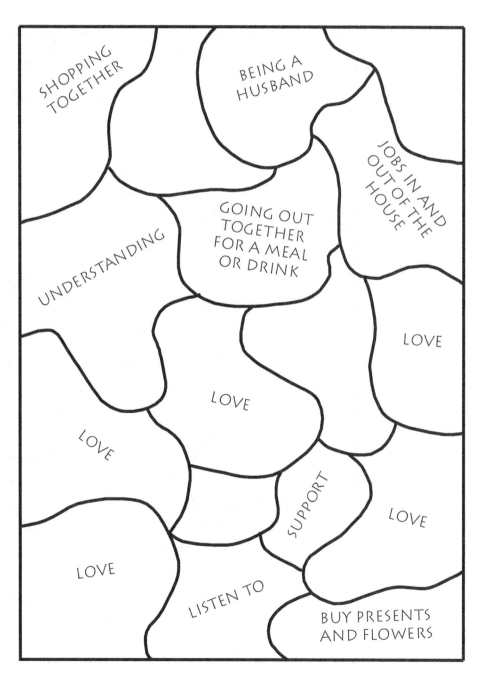

Figure 6.3: Bob's relationship jigsaw

In Bob's completed jigsaw (see Figure 6.3) it can be seen that he has left some gaps, there are also a number of repeated pieces (i.e. five pieces with 'love' on) and other pieces that Anne felt were learned by rote by Bob as opposed to being genuinely felt. By contrast, Anne's jigsaw (see Figure 6.4) is complete in that it has no gaps and it is comprehensive in terms of the range of emotions and enduring, positive features that it contains.

The direct outcome of completing this last task was that Bob was overwhelmed by Anne's view of what a relationship such as theirs should and could look like. He had never before realised there was so much to a marriage or a relationship! This last strategy seemed to be the catalyst that

Figure 6.4: Anne's relationship jigsaw

kick-started Bob into wanting to talk more with Anne. That's not to say that communication is at the level that Anne might have wished when she met Bob, but new rules, guidelines, boundaries, call them what you will, have been established between the clients and there is a real potential for things to improve between them. Counselling for these clients was concluded at this time to allow them to practice and consolidate their new-found skills.

Case study 2 – Barbara and Chris

It will be remembered that Barbara was a retired librarian and Chris a retired master builder who had often worked away on long contracts. Although she had always thought him a bit quirky at times, only since Chris's retirement did Barbara really consider his behaviour to be odd. According to Barbara, Chris (who had not been formally diagnosed with AS, but accepted displaying many of the traits) could not complete tasks at home that she thought were well within the compass of his abilities at work, namely:

- getting any practical task around the house completed – any communication around this usually resulted in a row

- planning specific events was also a problem, i.e. holidays, visits, outings etc., and

- the couple spent little or no time together doing couple things.

Strategy 1

In response to the first of the above issues, and given Chris's background in the building trade, it seemed likely that he might respond to a form of plan or diagram that wasn't so specific that it had to entail precise details, or even apply directly to the job in hand, but was general in the way the job was approached and continued. Accordingly the 'Task Planning' strategy was devised (see Handout 6.4) so that a task or job could be identified and spoken about by the couple, and they could discuss it again to clarify things without either party feeling they were either being got at or were getting at their partner. Any queries or problems about the task could be asked by way of the 5WH principle (What, When, Where, Who, Why and How), which should pretty well cover any eventuality. Timescales were also an important part of this strategy as Chris often started a job, but either started a second one before the first was finished or finished the first one much later than planned or not at all. The cyclical nature of this strategy allowed for an agreed check to happen to see how the task was going and for it to be spoken about again if necessary.

Strategy 2

In keeping with the 5WH principle, Barbara and Chris's second strategy was also formed around this. The 'Event Planning' document (see Handout 6.5) enabled the couple to think well ahead (always important to an AS person) about where they might go on holiday or when they might visit their grown-up children and their families situated in various parts of the UK, or how they might arrange a night out at the cinema or theatre. Certainly, by sitting together and creating their own 5WH questions and then working together towards answering them, the opportunity was there for better communication to take place.

Strategy 3

Planning, or rather the lack of it, seemed to be at the root of most of Barbara and Chris's problems. In a simple form of equation, 'Better Planning + More Talking = Improved Communication'. This next strategy, 'Daily Timetable' (see Handout 6.6) is simplicity itself, which is very often the best policy with AS people and indeed anyone else. After all, why complicate things if they can be conceived and put into practice in simple, functional ways. As can be seen (Figure 6.5) the timetable is divided into three columns, one for Barbara, one for Chris and a third one in the centre for them to do things together. It was felt important to allow the clients to be able to do things individually as well as together so that a balance remained in the relationship between autonomy and intimacy; their need to be individuals as well as part of a couple. The trick, of course, is to try to ensure that there is a balance and that the needs of the individual don't outweigh the needs of the couple or vice versa.

The other aspect of this strategy is the time zones. These came about as a result of various things such as when Barbara and Chris got up in the morning or went to bed at night, but these can be easily adjusted to suit the needs of other couples around working hours, children's schooling, etc. It will be noted from Figure 6.5 that the last entry at night before the couple went to bed was an agreement to discuss what they wanted to do the following day. Whilst strategies like this can be really useful, it is important to remember that any strategy or task should be non-intrusive. Indeed, Strategy 4 was devised specifically because of this.

Strategy 4

This strategy of a weekly timetable (see Handout 6.7) is merely an extension of the previous one, but came about because after a while Barbara and Chris did begin to feel that doing a timetable every night for the following day was becoming a bit 'challenging'. That said, it worked for the time that it had to before some fine-tuning became necessary. This replacement weekly timetable allowed the clients to feel less threatened by what, for them, had become an intrusive routine, but still kept them on board with thinking and talking about doing things as a couple. For other couples, Strategy 3 may be just what they need and feel comfortable with.

Barbara and Chris – Daily Timetable   **Date:** _____

Barbara	Together	Chris
Do a bit of ironing 9.00 a.m. – 11 a.m.	*Have breakfast together*	*Take care of the post*
   11 a.m. – 2 p.m.	*Go into town and do a bit of shopping*	
   2 p.m. – 6 p.m.	*Have lunch at the market café* *Do some gardening*	
Read my book for a while 6 p.m. – Bedtime	*Watch TV together, then talk about tomorrow*	*Finish grouting the tiles*

Figure 6.5

A review of Barbara and Chris's strategies

These four strategies were simple in design, easy and practical to use and yet allowed Barbara and Chris to communicate about anything and everything from going on holiday abroad to watching TV together, and from doing DIY jobs at home to having some lunch at the local market café; all of this and planning to do things for themselves as individuals as well. Chris said, 'I've never really felt comfortable communicating with people other than about work issues, and I've always found it difficult to talk about sensitive or emotional things. But the task planning sheet made me feel that we could talk about things without me feeling criticised.' He went on to say, 'The event planning and the timetables, particularly once we had changed from a daily to a weekly timetable, gave me the opportunity to think and talk with Barbara in advance about doing things, and for us then to actually do them together.'

Case study 3 – Carol and Doug

In his working capacity as a fireman, Doug (with a formal diagnosis of AS) was competent, assertive, forward thinking and very responsible. At home, however, he seemed to exist by a completely different set of rules; he lacked confidence, at times he was unassuming to the point of being almost inconspicuous, and he could seldom be trusted with even the simplest of tasks. Carol, a former Nurse, had initially been attracted to Doug because he had displayed his 'fireman' characteristics when they first met. Now she could not understand why the man she had married was no more, and how he could seemingly change from one character to another in the time it took him to get from work to home! Carol felt that if the following issues could be addressed, they might have a future together:

- Carol wanted Doug to take responsibility for doing things – preferably without having to be asked – and for him not to forget to do them once he had agreed.

- She also wanted Doug to be more communicative; he never volunteered information about anything and only spoke to her in response to things she said.

- She wanted more intimacy in their relationship as opposed to the current situation where it sometimes felt that she was the parent and he was the child.

Strategy 1

Carol and Doug's first strategy (see Figure 6.6) was a tried and tested one for many people and its regular usage in many homes speaks volumes for

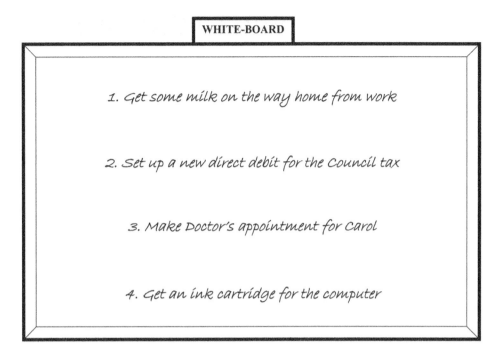

Figure 6.6

its effectiveness; it was a 'white-board' (a cork notice board could be used if preferred), on which messages and reminders could be written for actions that Doug had agreed to be responsible for. These actions ranged in their level of responsibility from buying some milk to making appointments for Carol at the doctor's surgery; from getting a new cartridge for the computer printer to setting up a new direct debit. The white-board was placed on the wall in the kitchen where Doug would see it numerous times every day and it would act as a constant reminder to him to fulfil his obligations.

Strategies 2 and 3

These two strategies (see Handouts 6.8 and 6.9) were used in conjunction with one another to address Carol's wish that Doug could communicate with her more easily. Doug said, 'It isn't that I don't want to talk to Carol, I'm just never quite sure of what to say – I don't seem to be able to think of anything and when I do it sounds a bit feeble.' The idea behind the first of these: 'Write Carol's Notes' (Figure 6.7) was that Doug never told Carol about anything that happened during his working day. He would come home and never volunteer anything – she would ask how his day went and he would just say 'Fine' or 'OK', which Carol found frustrating, but also (as we've heard before) very excluding. On this document, a copy of which Doug agreed to have with him every day at work, he would make a few

WRITE CAROL'S NOTES

WRITE CAROL'S NOTES

WRITE CAROL'S NOTES

WRITE CAROL'S NOTES

WRITE CAROL'S NOTES

Figure 6.7

Family questions

How are you?

•

How are the kids?

•

How did it go with daughter/son at ......

•

What have you been doing?

•

What have your mum and dad been doing?

Domestic questions

Is there any post?

•

Has anyone been around?

•

Have there been any phone calls?

•

Are there any e-mails?

Work statements

I'm working with .... today

•

We've dealt with .... so far today

•

The result of that job was ....

•

It's been good/boring/interesting/slow today

Personal statements

I'm looking forward to seeing you and the kids

•

You / daughter/son made me feel proud because ....

•

I'd like us to go for a walk/drink/the cinema

•

Talk about mum, dad, brothers, sisters

Figure 6.8

simple notes about the various events and happenings that he thought Carol might like to know about.

The reason the heading is repeated several times down the page is because early on in the use of this strategy, Doug had the piece of paper folded up in his tunic pocket. He thought it was just a blank piece of paper and threw it away. However, with 'Write Carol's Notes' printed on both sides of the paper, no matter how you fold it, it doesn't appear blank!

This couple's third strategy, 'Question Cards' (see Figure 6.8), came out of a couple of solo sessions I'd had with Doug when it felt appropriate and necessary to revert to Stage Two of the counselling model (individual counselling). During these sessions, done with Carol's approval, Doug told me, 'I always phone home when I'm at work, more because I think I should as opposed to having anything meaningful to say, but the conversations always seem to end quite quickly and awkwardly.' To try to combat this, Doug and I developed some questions around specific subjects, namely Family Questions, Domestic Questions, Work Statements and Personal Statements. I later created a separate card for Doug for each of these categories and by either randomly selecting one (e.g. by shuffling them) or by using them in rotation, Doug could pick a different subject to try to develop a conversation around every time he phoned Carol at home. I stressed to Doug that it wouldn't necessarily matter if the conversations were brief, the cards would assist him in making the phone calls and Carol would be pleased that he was engaging with her meaningfully. It was hoped that as time progressed, Doug would get used to making such telephone conversations and so the cards would ultimately be rendered obsolete.

Strategy 4

The last issue that Carol wanted to address was that of a lack of intimacy in her relationship with Doug. This final strategy, adapted from Maggie Scarf's second exercise in her book *Intimate Partners* (1988), was given to Carol and Doug for this purpose and was called 'Intimacy Task' (see Handout 6.10). This strategy is clearly outlined, with simple rules to follow, but with a clear objective that any requests for intimacy be modest and easily achievable and not too imposing or threatening to either party. Having such instructions was an advantage for Doug because he could refer to the rules of this task if he had any doubts about them. They were also useful for Carol because she could refer Doug to them if she thought he was misinterpreting them or not applying them properly.

A review of Carol and Doug's strategies

At first, the use of the white-board was something of a revelation. Sometimes Carol would suggest an action be included on the board and other times she would specifically ask Doug to add one. On other occasions he added actions to the board himself. However these actions came to be there, Doug seemed to relish taking them on. It was as if he really enjoyed performing more of a shared role in the relationship. However, taking one step too far, Doug attempted to fulfil this role without the use of the white-board and sadly slipped back into forgetting things. I asked him why he'd stopped using it, and much the same as Bob in Case study 1, he felt a bit inadequate in having to have written reminders to do things. I told Doug that I use reminders all of the time, either by writing them on my 'Things To Do List' or putting them on the 'Reminder Facility' on my mobile phone. This last suggestion seemed to appeal much more to Doug and by a bit of fine-tuning, a natural transition was made to the design of a strategy so that it better suited the individual.

By using Strategies 2 and 3 together, Doug became better at making telephone calls to Carol and at keeping her informed of things that had happened to him whilst at work. Indeed, Doug began using the idea of writing things down to assist him in other ways, e.g. if he was taking the car to the garage or getting a present for a birthday or anniversary, he would write down on a piece of paper what information he wanted to impart to the mechanic or the shop assistant respectively. The notion of having things written down privately for Doug (on paper, on his Question Cards or in his phone), seemed to appeal to him much more than having things 'publicly displayed', even if they were in his own kitchen! He continued using the Question Cards at work, but only on occasions when his mind was elsewhere.

Strategy 4 worked well for both partners, albeit I suspect for different reasons. I think it worked for Carol because she was happy to have Doug participate fully in meeting her intimacy requests and making his own, which she then met. I think Doug was able to make this strategy work because he knew that he was pleasing Carol by doing his part of it, but he didn't really understand why this 'game' of taking turns had the positive impact that it did!

Case study 4 – Diane and Eric

The issues with this couple were not particularly prevalent when it was just the two of them, but became very apparent after their daughter was born. As with lots of couples, they came to feel distant from one another. It was during this rocky period in their relationship that the AS behaviour (which both later realised had always been there at some level), became more obvious. They had spoken about Eric having AS and he was reluctant to be labelled. He did however, concede to having AS traits and was self-diagnosed to the point that he regarded himself as being different to other men when his behaviour was more extreme.

During my Stage Two talk with Diane she said, 'It's sometimes very difficult to discuss things with Eric as he talks at me rather than to me.' It was during his same-stage talk with me that Eric explained how difficult it was for him to engage socially. He said, 'People expect quick verbal responses, but I can't always process things that quickly and if I'm required to answer before I've really understood the essence of what has been said to me, then I'm inclined to say the wrong thing – which unfortunately happens quite often.' In keeping with most AS–NT couples, Diane and Eric described the essence of their problems as 'emotion versus logic'; Diane owning the emotional retorts and Eric accepting that he was logical to the point of frustrating Diane. Their desired outcomes from counselling were:

- for each to check things out before reacting negatively and to accept that they would both sometimes get things wrong

- to resolve the emotion versus logic issue such that each partner attended better to the other's needs whilst still having the freedom to express his or her own.

Strategy 1

The first thing to put into place for Diane and Eric seemed to be a 'Conflict Prevention Plan' (see Handout 6.11), which they were keen to implement straight away. This was a simple set of written rules such that when either of them felt upset, annoyed or just plain angry about something, or thought the other might be experiencing similar feelings, they could adopt the first level of the plan to express their concerns and so hopefully 'head off' any impending row. Of course, if there wasn't anything negative on either of their minds, then no harm was done in making a simple enquiry. However, if there was something troubling either of the partners, they could then go to the second level and arrange a suitable time for these negative issues to be discussed, perhaps allowing for a cooling-off period first. The third level of the plan tied in directly with their second strategy.

Strategy 2

This particular strategy, called 'Constructive Discussion' (see Handout 6.12) is a variation on a theme, loosely called 'Rules for Rows', and was given this name by Eric who preferred to think that they didn't row, they just had different ways of seeing the world (emotion versus logic). The beauty of this type of task is that every couple who decides to try it can adjust the rules to their own particular needs. It will be seen that there are some very precise features of Diane and Eric's version in that point 2 refers to the discussion being about 18 minutes long (not 15 or 20), and them having three minutes each to talk and be listened to. I know from discussing this with them that they thought three minutes was long enough for the talker to say what they had to without appearing to be moaning for the sake of it and also long enough for the non-talking partner to listen without saying anything. If the talking partner really did need more time then point 6 allowed for this, but usually the 18 minutes was stuck to, which meant the time for talking and listening was fairly and equally shared between them.

A review of Diane and Eric's strategies

Diane and Eric's responses to these two strategies were very rewarding for a couple therapist. Diane said, 'We've experienced a communication breakthrough since using these strategies. I certainly feel much happier now and there is a greater sense of trust between us.' Eric added, 'Communication between us has definitely improved and we're optimistic it will continue like this.'

Other strategies

In sharing with you these case studies, I've outlined several specific strategies that were used by these clients. As you will have seen, some of these remained in their original form, whilst others needed adjusting so the clients could make better use of them. Each strategy has the potential to be adapted if necessary. One couple adapted the 'What Colour Are You Feeling' task so that in addition to a mood being identified, a numbered scale from 0 to 10 was also added to determine the strength of that feeling. When the AS partner placed the appropriate mood card in the agreed place, the non-AS partner would ask, 'How strong is this feeling?' On the basis that 0 = weak and 10 = strong, the AS partner would then add the relevant number. If we were to exemplify this by using Bob's chart in Case study 1 and added the number 8 to his orange card, we would know he was feeling 'very sad'.

Another strategy, not hitherto mentioned, was designed around an AS man and his wife who shared similar communication difficulties to other couples because he could never discuss his problems with her face-to-face. The remedy was that they would talk to one another by phone from different rooms in the house. One might be concerned that this would run up an expensive phone bill, but there are ways to overcome this either by the brevity of the call, by using a phone extension (if there is one), or by texting each other on mobile phones as opposed to actually talking. This last idea can be extended to talking via the computer, by e-mailing or using the messenger facility.

I'm reminded of another of my couple clients who I became very fond of. They know who they are because I asked their permission to mention two particular strategies that they instituted themselves. When I first met them (and for some time after) they would often argue over the most innocuous things. Initially they failed to understand why this was happening, but as their knowledge of AS increased and they became more aware of its impact upon their relationship, so they were able to develop some interesting strategies of their own to either try to stop an argument occurring or to reconcile one when it had already happened. In an attempt to prevent arguments they co-wrote a manifesto that included how much they were committed to each other and how each would try to live up to this commitment and take responsibility for adhering to it. They each read their respective parts of the manifesto to each other every morning and every night. They say it is ill-advised to go to bed on an argument, but what a wonderful thing for any couple to be able to re-commit themselves to each other before they go to sleep at night and then again when they start a new day in the morning. Their second strategy, if an argument did ensue for any reason, was for one or other partner to take responsibility for placing a favourite teddy bear in an agreed place (perhaps the armchair in the lounge) to indicate that they wanted to make up. Given that visual messages work particularly well with AS people, this was a very well devised strategy for conveying something that otherwise might not have been communicated verbally, but nonetheless conveyed the message of wanting to make up very effectively.

The reality is that the types of strategies and their variations are endless. The only restriction to creating any number of strategies, lists, plans, rules and reminders are the limits of one's own imagination. There is another way of managing AS between partners that hasn't yet been mentioned, other than by me alluding to the need for autonomy as well as intimacy in a couple relationship. It isn't a strategy as such, but it is extremely important. I refer to the need for the non-AS partner in particular to have access to a support group where possible, and as an absolute necessity to have time for themselves, away from their partners. I also discuss the merits of the AS partner having these opportunities. It is to these two themes that the next chapter is given.

Chapter 6: Handouts

Handout 6.1   Blank Anger Scratchpad' to be photocopied by the counsellor for use by the clients

Handout 6.2   'What Colour Are You Feeling' chart to be photocopied by the counsellor for use by the clients

Handout 6.3   Blank 'Relationship Jigsaw' to be photocopied by the counsellor for use by the clients

Handout 6.4   'Task Planning' chart used in Case Study 2

Handout 6.5   'Event Planning' chart used in Case Study 2

Handout 6.6   Blank Couple 'Daily Timetable' to be photocopied by the counsellor for use by the clients

Handout 6.7   Blank Couple 'Weekly Timetable' to be photocopied by the counsellor for use by the clients

Handout 6.8   Blank Couple 'Write Notes' form to be photocopied by the counsellor for use by the clients

Handout 6.9   'Question Cards' used in Case Study 3 to be photocopied by the counsellor for use by the clients

Handout 6.10   'Intimacy Task' used in Case Study 3 to be photocopied by the counsellor for use by the clients

Handout 6.11   'Conflict Prevention Plan' used in Case Study 4 to be photocopied by the counsellor for use by the clients

Handout 6.12   'Constructive Discussion' used in Case Study 4 to be photocopied by the counsellor for use by the clients

✓

Handout 6.1: Anger Scratchpad

Me	Anne
Home	**Work**
Family	**Neighbours**
Other matters	**Other matters**

Handout 6.2: What Colour Are You Feeling?

Name:

Happy

Sad

Anxious

Excited

Depressed

Confident

Worried

Secure

Insecure

Positive

Angry

Tearful

Uncertain

Handout 6.3: Relationship Jigsaw

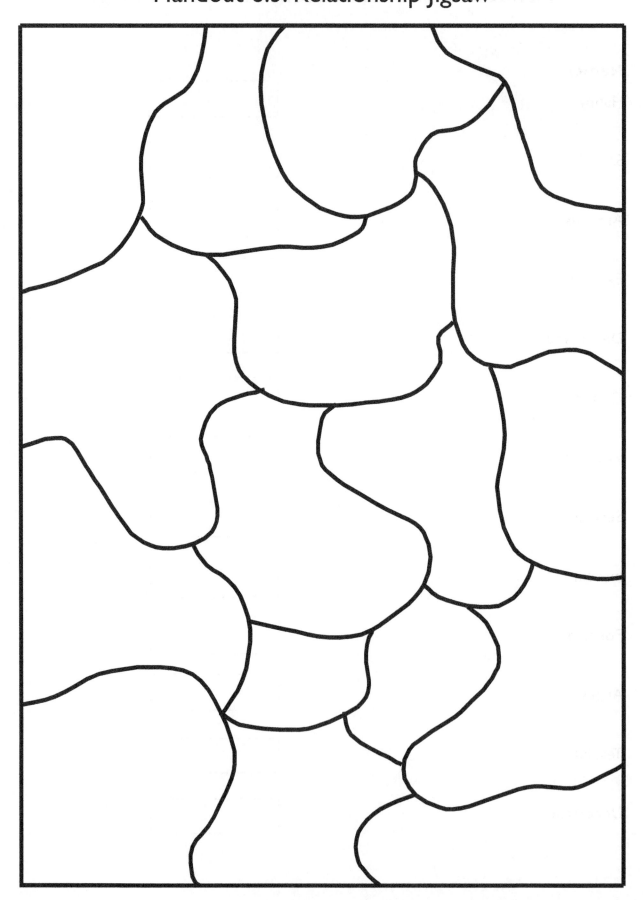

Handout 6.4: Task Planning

Be clear about the task

Talk over the task again if necessary

Ask questions to clarify exactly what needs to be done

5WH

Consider timescales

Check how the task is going

Handout 6.5: Event Planning

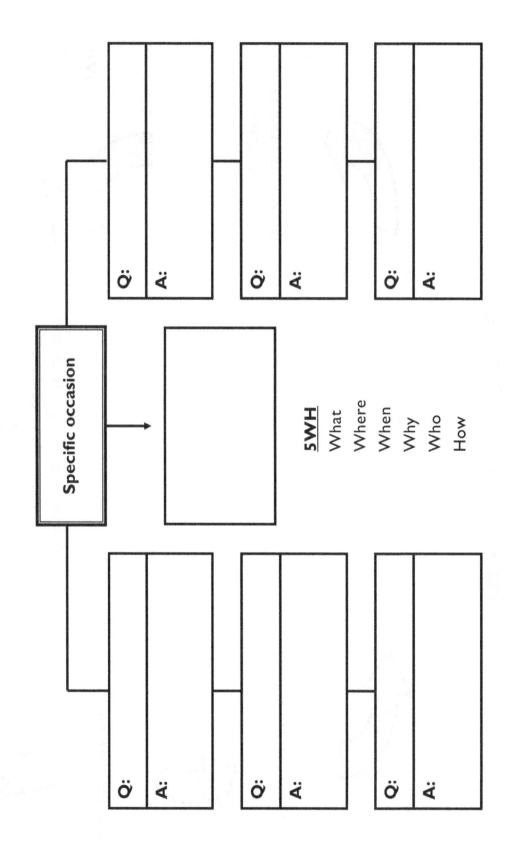

Specific occasion

5WH
What
Where
When
Why
Who
How

Q:
A:

Q:
A:

Q:
A:

Q:
A:

Q:
A:

Q:
A:

Handout 6.6: Couple – Daily Timetable

Date: _____

Her	*Together*	*Him*
9.00 a.m. – 11 a.m.		
11 a.m. – 2 p.m.		
2 p.m. – 6 p.m.		
6 p.m. – Bedtime		

Handout 6.7: Couple – Weekly Timetable

Week commencing _____

Her	Together	Him
	Monday	
	Tuesday	
	Wednesday	
	Thursday	
	Friday	
	Saturday	
	Sunday	

WRITE NOTES

WRITE NOTES

WRITE NOTES

WRITE NOTES

WRITE NOTES

Handout 6.9: Question Cards

Family questions

How are you?

•

How are the kids?

•

How did it go with
daughter/son at ......

•

What have you been
doing?

•

What have your mum and
dad been doing?

Domestic questions

Is there any post?

•

Has anyone been
around?

•

Have there been any
phone calls?

•

Are there any
e-mails?

Work statements

I'm working with ....
today

•

We've dealt with ....
so far today

•

The result of that job
was ....

•

It's been good/boring/
interesting/slow today

Personal statements

I'm looking forward to
seeing you and the kids

•

You / daughter/son made
me feel proud
because ....

•

I'd like us to go for a walk/
drink/the cinema

•

Talk about mum, dad,
brothers, sisters

Handout 6.10: Intimacy Task

The instructions for this task are as follows; the couple agree to divide the weekdays between them. One partner may, for example, take Monday, Wednesday and Friday, whilst the other partner takes Tuesday, Thursday and Saturday. On Sunday, their day off, they are free to let their old behavioural cycle run its familiar course.

On the odd days of the week (one, three and five) the first partner is in charge of the intimacy in the relationship. On the even days (two, four and six) the other partner is given control of the intimacy. On their respective days, each partner makes one intimacy request, the other partner having agreed to participate (more than one request can be made by agreement of the partners in the normal course of life, but are outside of the bounds of this task). These are the relatively simple, non-threatening rules.

It is important to add that each partner's intimacy requests must be achievable – that is, not 'love me forever' or something similar. The intimacy request should be on the relatively modest side and some-thing practicable and possible at that time or soon after. It should be clearly described in terms of something behavioural, something that a partner *can* do, e.g. 'I would like you to come with me for a walk'. Or 'Can you massage my neck/back', or 'Let me choose the movie/video we see tonight'.

Caution should be taken not to select intimate requests that will produce conflict in the partner, or that cannot be met when, for example, the responding partner is just about to leave home to go to work or meet an appointment.

Handout 6.11: Conflict Prevention Plan

For each partner to restrict their negative comments and try to check with one another about any concerns or frustrations.

1st level: For either partner to be able to say, 'I'm feeling angry/annoyed/upset, can we talk about it...?'

OR

'You seem quiet/upset/troubled, can we talk about it...?'

2nd level: For the clients to agree a time to discuss any issues that may exist (allowing time for any negative feelings to subside).

3rd level: To discuss the issues by listening, talking and sharing (see Handout 6.12 'Constructive Discussion').

Handout 6.12: Constructive Discussion

In a *constructive* talk:

1. We choose the best time and place (if possible don't go to bed on a row).

2. Allow about 18 minutes initially – then agree how much time on future occasions.

3. Talk about the relevant issues; where other issues may arise these can be accommodated on future occasions.

4. Time out during the session is an option if either party feels the need.

5. No silent treatment, withdrawing from each other or 'door slamming', etc.

6. The timing should be fairly and equally shared. At the end of that time the listener asks, 'Do you need more time?' Each partner should talk in terms of 'I feel…', 'I need…', 'I hope…', not 'You did this…', 'You said that…' etc.

7. Don't use the three minutes to 'have a go', try to learn to listen to each other and share feelings with one another.

Chapter 7

Stage Seven: Ongoing Support and Personal Space

A true friend unbosoms freely, advises justly, assists readily, adventures boldly, takes all patiently, defends courageously, and continues a friend unchangeably.

William Penn

Part 1

There are two key elements essential to this part of my counselling model and I will be expounding on these as if they were separate and distinct elements, but it is my view that they should run concurrently with one another if possible, each thereby adding more weight and purpose to the other. It is also important to add that although this chapter represents Stage Seven of the model, the two elements it contains could (and should, where possible) be put into place at the earliest opportunity.

Part 1 of this chapter will deal with the first of these elements, which is the process of support. I will talk about support for both the NT partner and the AS partner, where it can be sought, the various forms it can take and who can provide it. The reader will recall from Chapter 1 that I first encountered the suggestion of support for non-AS partners from the research that I did into how counselling had benefited (or not as the case may be) AS–NT couples who had already received couple counselling. Part 2 will deal with the second element, that of the personal space and the freedom to allow both the NT and AS partners to be who they want to be, but in the context of balancing this with the intimacy necessary for the survival of the relationship.

The first type of support function I want to talk about is that which can be provided for the neurotypical partner in an AS–NT relationship. One of the great difficulties for NT partners is having no one to share the burden of their Asperger experiences with. It is one thing to share such experiences with family and friends (of which I will say more later), but crucially, these people are unlikely to know about AS. They won't know of the apparent lack of concern displayed by an AS partner; the seemingly uncaring, selfish attitude of a man who has to rigidly apply his own set of rules to everyday life at the expense of anybody and everybody else. Neither will they know of the confusion that faces the NT partner when this AS man shows he can be gentle, open and honest, committed and sincere at the same time as being so difficult to live with. The only people who are likely to understand what it is like to experience these distinct, diverse and challenging emotions are other NT wives and partners. If sought after and provided in the right way, it is these people coming together as groups that can provide vital support for one another.

Client-based NT support groups

How then does one NT wife or partner locate another one when it is difficult beyond imagination for couples to even find a couple counsellor or therapist that specialises in AS? (I know of only a few dotted around the country, if there are others out there, I tender my apologies, but it still leaves us very thin on the ground.) Where partners in an AS–NT relationship are fortunate enough to be seeing an Asperger counsellor, herein lies one answer to obtaining group support.

I am personally familiar with two such groups, albeit run on quite different lines. In my own practice working with Asperger couples, I came to know about a group of women that came up with the idea of starting their own self-help support group for NT partners. A leaflet was designed advertising the existence of this group, containing contact details, which then through me was made available to other NT partners. I stress at this point that I didn't actively involve myself in the group, I merely told people of its existence. A number of other wives and partners subsequently contacted the group and agreed to meet on different occasions, sometimes in pairs, often in small groups, sometimes for a coffee morning, sometimes whilst having a meal out, but always to share their experiences and hear how they compared with one another's. In this way the partners could feel they were not alone with their problems, but could share coping strategies or could agree to phone one another if and when the need arose.

Another such group for NT partners existed directly around the counselling practice the clients attended as couples. This particular group also met for coffee mornings, and they shared their experiences with one another as did the first group, but there were fundamental differences between the two groups. The meetings of this second group were restricted to being held at the clinic where the counselling took place and so there was no social outlet as such to speak of. They were also arranged on a regular, timetabled basis and, importantly, these meetings were facilitated by their counsellor. This last factor could prove to be an important one because the potential exists, understandably, for NT partners to want to offload their negative experiences to their peers, but these negative things can easily become the predominant issue and the whole feeling of the meeting could become a negative experience as opposed to the positive one it was supposed to be. Where an experienced counsellor facilitates the meeting, this is less likely to happen.

Geographically located NT support

I have also had the opportunity to help the NT partners of my clients get together 'geographically' because of where they live in relation to one another. On these occasions I have merely acted as a go-between in that one NT client will have asked me if there were any other Asperger clients that I was seeing from the general area in which they live. In these situations, when seeing clients (assuming they were current clients at that time) I have simply asked the NT partner if they would be prepared to be contacted by the NT wife or partner of another of my clients. If the response was positive, I would get permission for their respective telephone numbers to be released to each other and then leave the rest up to them. I'm pleased to say I've had some quite positive feedback about such relationships being formed. Even if clients have concluded with counselling and are no longer seeing me, there still exists the opportunity to write to them to ask if they would be willing to meet with other clients or ex-clients in their area.

On other occasions I have been contacted by people from different parts of the country where there is no provision at all for counselling couples where AS is a presenting issue, and it is simply too far and too expensive for people to travel to Coventry to see me on an ongoing counselling basis (albeit some people have travelled from as far afield as the south coast of England, South Wales and the north of England for one-off sessions). Where such long distances are involved, it has not been unusual for me to engage with these people on a telephone or e-mail counselling basis. Here again, I have been asked to initiate contact between geographically located NT partners and, with due respect to ethical principles, I have willingly obliged.

However people come together to provide support for one another, it is important during those difficult periods in their lives to have somebody available to share their experiences with that they can relate to. In the context of an NT–NT relationship one would hope that this sharing and support would be mutually available between the partners, but having someone who understands what it is like to experience an AS–NT relationship that is different in so many ways, and who can provide the right kind of support to steer them through the difficult times, is invaluable. So with all of these various ways of linking NT partners together geographically, the potential exists for the right kind of support to be available and the positive prospects for such networking are obvious. Care still has to be taken though, to avoid the pitfalls of engendering a negative structure where the only things that get shared are critical comments about respective AS spouses, and the only 'support' received may be that which damages one's own relationship even further.

Support available from websites

I want to turn now to a different type of support altogether, namely that which can be obtained for both AS and NT partners (or indeed AS people who are not in a relationship) via the websites of organisations such as the National Autistic Society, Autism West Midlands (in my own region), Edinburgh Lothian Asperger Society (ELAS), the Asperger Society and Families of Adults Affected by Asperger Syndrome (FAAAS), to name but a few. Contact details for these organisations and others either regionally based in the United Kingdom, or in the United States and Canada, can be easily located either direct via their respective websites (see the References section at the end of the book) or via a good computer search engine. I want now to briefly look at these organisations to indicate the various and comprehensive services they provide.

The National Autistic Society is the largest organisation of its kind in the United Kingdom and provides a wide range of services for people with autistic spectrum disorders and their families. These services include, amongst many, social skills programmes for children and adults, a diagnostic and advice centre for children and adults with social and communication problems, access to further education courses, advice in securing and maintaining employment as well as vocational training.

There are many regional organisations that deal with autistic spectrum disorders, and in my view Autism West Midlands is a standard bearer because of the diversity and quality of the services they provide. As well as providing pupils with residential and daytime educational facilities and adults with full-time residential care, there is specialist supported living and employment support for adults with Asperger Syndrome. ASSET (Asperger Syndrome Support and Enablement Team) works within the community as an outreach service to help people with an autistic spectrum disorder gain life skills and social skills. Another outreach service, ASPIRE (Asperger Syndrome People into Real Employment), provides employment training and support for people with AS and also training for employers to help people with AS in the workplace.

Autism West Midlands has also been responsible for setting up a Criminal Justice Forum that involves members from their own community, the police, Crown Prosecution Service, probation service, the prison service, NACRO (the crime reduction charity), the British Institute of Learning Difficulties and many others. Its aim is to raise awareness of the difficulties that face people with an autistic spectrum disorder if and when they become involved in the criminal justice system in this country, be they a victim, witness or offender. Such awareness has been raised through the specific training of police officers, solicitors and other professionals in the legal system, by staging conferences and workshops and, importantly, by the introduction of an Asperger Identification Card that the AS person can carry with them and produce to someone in authority if they get into difficulties with the criminal justice system. This card will have on it the name of the AS person to whom it has been allocated as well as a responsible adult that the AS person would wish to be contacted in such circumstances.

Moving now to north of the border, ELAS is the Edinburgh Lothian Asperger Society. This group was set up quite recently (its constitution was adopted in May 2003) as a social outlet for adults aged 18 and above who have AS or, indeed, people who *may* have AS, but have yet to be formally diagnosed. The partners or friends of AS people are also able to attend. Their purpose is to give AS people, their partners and friends an opportunity to meet alike people and participate in social events with them. They also hold discussion evenings and often have visiting speakers who talk about issues relevant to the group. Their primary purpose, as quoted on their website, is 'to provide an opportunity for people with AS to accept, value, support and encourage one another'.

I want to conclude this section by mentioning two other AS support organisations that are located in the United States. The first of these is the Asperger Society, founded in 2004 and is based in San Francisco, California. The group's founders are Paul Bondonno and Isaac Knight, both of whom have AS. The successful approach adopted by this group is one where AS children and adolescents are mentored by AS adults who have been successful in their own walks of life, but still have all of the experiences of growing up with AS. This group also facilitates a programme for children and adults to develop and flourish in both education and the workplace. Since 2004 the Asperger Society has spread its wings and is now expanding into areas of southern California.

The FAAAS is based in Massachusetts, and is the last of the websites that I want to share with you. The mission statement on their website offers support to the families of adults with AS. Their goals include educating the public about AS in the adult population and raising awareness in the medical communities as to how this disorder affects not only the individuals who have it, but also the extent to which the lives of the families of these people are affected. As their title indicates, this organisation is one where the emphasis of their support is directed towards AS people in the adult population.

Meeting up with other people who understand AS issues can be so important during the difficult times in an AS–NT relationship, but even if times are not so difficult, the fellowship that these organisations provide is immeasurable. For those people who are unable to attend such organisations locally, the amount of knowledge, experience and guidance to be found through their websites is both vast and invaluable.

Support from family and friends

I am reminded of certain couples who have been my clients who had issues of one form or another that related to their families or friends. Some had negative experiences with their extended families or friends that unfortunately impacted upon their own relationship, whilst others had more rewarding experiences from which everyone benefited.

One such couple was Ian and Lucy who had been married for nearly three years when they came to see me. Ian had no siblings and his parents lived in Scotland. Lucy had an older sister and three older brothers who had all cosseted her as the baby of the family, which to some extent had continued even after she had married Ian. When Ian and Lucy were courting one another there were no signs of the problems that were to follow (as we know, this is often the case). After they were married, however, Ian's behaviour changed and he became seemingly indifferent and cold towards Lucy and the first signs of marital disharmony became evident. In the bosom of her close-knit family, Lucy's marital plight became a topic of discussion and Ian, understandably from what was known at that time, was very soon the recipient of some scathing criticism by Lucy's family. The best advice her family could offer to Lucy was to leave Ian and start divorce proceedings.

Lucy was not prepared to give up so easily on the man she loved and so she sought advice from her GP as to Ian's behaviour. A quick chain of events then followed in that the GP described AS to Lucy who in turn explained it to Ian. He subsequently underwent a formal diagnosis and was found to have AS. It was at this time that they agreed to have counselling and were referred to me.

The reader might imagine at this point that Lucy's family would be only too pleased to receive an explanation for Ian's behaviour and to learn that he and Lucy were working as a couple to overcome their difficulties. Not at all. Instead of rewarding her commitment to her marriage they continued to try to convince her to leave Ian. The last time I saw Ian and Lucy, relations were still strained between them and her family. But Lucy had in effect 'grown up' and relinquished her baby role. Despite the powerful negative influence of Lucy's family, she and Ian are still married and now have a baby son.

How sad it is that Lucy's family couldn't see the potential for hers and Ian's relationship after his diagnosis. One can understand their concerns when it was thought that Ian had rejected Lucy, but when an explanation did come along for his behaviour they were too short-sighted to see beyond the problems or to take the time to learn that an AS man can have many endearing features, such as honesty, commitment, reliability and faithfulness. For my own part I feel that a large part of the problem was the inability of Lucy's family to let go of her as the 'baby' of the family, but their reluctance to do so ultimately led to them losing Lucy altogether.

In stark contrast to the lack of support by Lucy's family is the experience of Alison, who with her husband Rick, were also my clients. Everything seemed ok with Alison and Rick until their little girl was born. It was then that Rick changed and appeared not to be able to relate to either Alison or their daughter. He had lost his role as husband and didn't know how to fulfil his new dual roles of husband and father. Naturally, Alison's family were concerned, as were Rick's, all of whom lived fairly locally to the couple. It was Rick who went to see their GP on the advice of his parents, and after an appropriate referral he was diagnosed as having AS.

One of the difficulties Alison and Rick imagined they would have in coming to see me was their need for a babysitter. Not a problem! Between both of their families and their close friends, the support they received was excellent. What Alison and Rick decided to do to reciprocate this support was to share the knowledge they gradually gained about AS with their families and friends, so as to keep them updated with everything. If I gave Alison and Rick certain reading material I thought would help them, so their families and friends read it too. As Alison and Rick learnt new strategies to overcome certain difficulties, so did everyone close to them.

What a difference this support made to this young couple. Instead of the gulf that appeared between them widening, it was bridged by the support they received. Instead of feeling isolated and apart from everyone, they felt included and cared about. The difference in the levels of support received by these two young couples; from non-existent to loving and caring, was tangibly obvious just by observing them. Lucy and Ian came through things in their own way, but were isolated from Lucy's family, whilst Alison and Rick achieved so much more by virtue of the support they received from their families and friends.

Support inclined more towards the AS partner

I started off this chapter by talking about the support that is (or can be) available for NT partners, before explaining the support that is mutually available to NT and AS partners via websites, families and friends, and of course between the couple. I now want to mention the support that is available that is more inclined towards AS partners and which builds into the second part of this chapter by giving both the AS and NT partners the time and space to be their own person.

At the risk of leaving some groups out, I want to mention two particular types of support group available for people with AS. In citing the first of these I turn once again to Autism West Midlands. They run social groups for individuals with AS that meet regularly whereby the members take turns to select the activity that the group undertakes, and in so doing the AS members have the opportunity to engage with people outside of their family circle. Autism West Midlands also run a number of discussion groups for AS people throughout Birmingham and Worcester that meet on a monthly basis to discuss various topics, and then have a meal out at a restaurant or pub afterwards.

In Coventry, there is a group designed to raise awareness of AS that caters for people with AS and their families and friends. By virtue of the syndrome affecting more men than women, the group comprises mainly men who meet once a month to create a support structure in which they feel secure and validated. The group was originally facilitated by the Coventry Social Services, and indeed is still funded by them, but they are now a self-help group as they manage and administer their own affairs. Given the difficulties that people with AS have in communicating and socialising, it is to the credit of this group (and Social Services for continuing to fund them) that they organise themselves in the way they do. The members are a shining example to other AS people because they demonstrate that the life skills and management skills necessary to manage their own support group are within their capabilities, if only somebody takes the time to help them discover and nurture these. Whilst it is accepted that some AS people will never be sufficiently independent to cope with life skills and management skills to this extent, the fact that there are AS people who can, who will assist AS people who can't, is a wonderful example of what true community spirit is all about. For this particular group the initial support came from the Social Services who helped the group discover the skills that existed within their membership; who nurtured these skills and then came to realise that the group was strong enough and capable enough to take care of itself.

Part 2

Let all your views in life be directed to a solid,
however moderate, independence; without it no man
can be happy, nor even honest.

Junius

If a relationship between two people is to remain a wholesome one, then I propose there ought to be a healthy balance between the intimacy and the autonomy that each partner is able to demonstrate and that the relationship is able to contain (see Figure 7.1). Intimacy keeps the love in the relationship working and autonomy retains one's sense of personal identity. The balance between these two entities is a personal arrangement between the couple. Some people enjoy being wrapped up in the company of their partner, whilst others may feel emotionally smothered if they are integrated to the point of having no personal space or freedom to be themselves and to make their own choices.

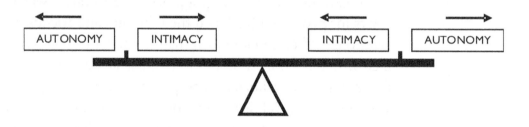

Figure 7.1: Relationship see-saw

Not only is there a intensity level at which these entities can function, but there may well be a variance over time, e.g. when couples first start courting they may be in each other's presence at every opportunity, but as time goes on and the relationship becomes more emotionally secure, the need to be in the constant physical presence of each other can be replaced by knowing that your loved one is with you in mind and spirit, if not in body. As an example of this spiritual closeness, if I go away with some friends for an overnight stay or perhaps a couple of nights away, my wife and I will naturally miss one another, but the fact that I will have gone on such a trip with her blessing provides for a feeling of emotional and spiritual connectedness that compensates for our lack of being together physically.

However, some people, and more usually those in AS–NT relationships, are not always as fortunate in having this type of arrangement. Almost without exception, the NT partners in the couples I meet complain of AS monopolising their lives. At the point of entering the counselling process everything to them seems to revolve around their husband's or partner's needs. It is very often the NT partner who has to take responsibility for doing something that may be important to the family (but not the AS partner), or else it doesn't get done. The view that it is the NT partner who has to learn to think like her AS husband is little comfort on top of everything else that she has to be accountable and responsible for. Having a partner with AS can become so all consuming, so constraining that it feels to the NT partner as if she is being suffocated and cannot breathe. It literally takes over every aspect of her life. The AS partner may not understand why things are as they are in their relationship, but his partner's unhappiness will inevitably affect him and make him unhappy also. So what then is the remedy to this intense feeling of having your life and your identity taken from you?

Let me take you back to the comment made by one of my research subjects in Chapter 1 and remind you that this was made by an AS husband and not an NT wife. He said, 'A support group for my wife would be very helpful.' Another of my research subjects who was also a husband with AS said, 'We now do certain activities separately. She needed to do things for herself and has become more of a person in her own right, but our relationship has benefited from this also.' These AS husbands both realised the need for their NT wives to be away from them, to exercise their choice to do something for themselves even if only for a short period of time, and for that time to be unburdened by AS. However, this situation is a far cry from the more usual ones where the AS partner doesn't acknowledge or even realise that such a need for his NT partner exists.

I believe the key to this dilemma lies largely in the 'when' as opposed to the 'how' individual time is spent. Let me explain. Many NT partners understandably complain that their AS partners spend inordinate amounts of time involving themselves in what some people might refer to as an obsession. For my own part I feel it is much healthier, and usually more accurate to refer to these obsessions as special interests. Commonly, a lot of AS men like to participate in anything to do with computers, others may like to involve themselves quite intensely in gardening or DIY (the NT reader may now be thinking 'I should be so lucky!'). The point is that a special interest can be literally anything, but the problem is not so much *how* the AS partner fulfils his special interest rather than *when* does he do it and for how long will it keep him away from his NT spouse and/or their children?

This is where the therapy comes in. As I see it there are two basic scenarios we can attempt to establish between the partners, so that both feel they have the time and space to do their own thing (autonomy) whilst also attempting to engender more quality time together (intimacy). The first of these is that the AS partner does his thing, be it computing, astronomy, or researching the First World War, for a set amount of time in any one day or week, whilst in parallel with this the NT partner takes the time she needs each day or week to do whatever she wants to do. In this way they are simultaneously committed to their own needs and some sense of parity is achieved in the length of time committed to their individual pursuits. There may be problems associated with this scenario if the couple have young children and require babysitting arrangements. The second scenario is that the partners arrange different times of the day or week to partake in their own thing (which would take care of the babysitting arrangements, but allows less time together), but they should still try to ensure that the time spent on their respective pursuits suits both of their needs. Now I am aware that this second option almost sounds like a formula for living separate lives. The cautionary note that I add to implementing any strategy or change in lifestyle is that of managing the change so that the individual partners and the relationship benefit.

What is crucially important is that the rules for these arrangements are written down in some way, perhaps in the form of a 'contract' signed by both partners or by using either the Daily Timetable shown in Handout 6.6 or the Weekly Timetable in Handout 6.7 (Chapter 6), or indeed a combination of a written agreement and the timetable. By using these strategies in conjunction with a written agreement, the partners can keep a check on the time each gives to their own interests and to their partner and the process can be jointly managed to achieve a successful outcome. By working together in this way the potential for conflict in the relationship is reduced and there is also an opportunity for the partners to spend more quality time together.

For some AS–NT couples (such as my two research guys and their wives), an arrangement to equalise the time to follow their respective interests is relatively easy to put in place. The obvious reward for the NT partners is that they get the personal space and time to be themselves with the added bonus that this time is indeed 'Asperger free'. Sometimes the benefit of having a better relationship from these arrangements can be remuneration enough for some AS partners, but for others it may not be quite that easy. If an arrangement requires that the AS partner has to give up some of his special interest time in order that the couple spend more time together, there often has to be some more tangible form of reward in place for the AS partner before he will even consider giving up any of what he considers to be 'his time'. In these circumstances there might have to be some form of negotiation around what that reward might be. A reward can take many forms, but it has to appear to the AS partner that their world has changed for the better because of it. Rewards can include the following:

- some agreed time for the AS partner to talk to his spouse about his special interest

- some agreed, but limited participation by the NT partner in the AS partner's special interest

- an agreement to assist the AS partner during periods of stress or high anxiety.

Such rewards could also include:

- an agreement that there would be less criticism of the AS partner because the NT partner now has access to her own space and time

- a less anxious existence because both partners are getting time to do what they want

- perhaps an agreement that the AS partner doesn't have to participate in something that they really don't like doing.

The opportunities for generating rewards are many and varied, but will depend on several factors, including the nature and intensity of the AS partner's special interest, the amount of time given to it, the type of relationship the couple have and how significantly the AS impacts upon it and many, many more. I say to the NT reader, you know your AS partner better than anyone else does and you know what he might respond to in order for you to broker such a time-sharing arrangement.

I hope I have shown in this chapter the opportunities and the benefits that exist for both AS and NT partners in seeking for themselves the various forms of support that are available to them. I also hope that the notion of a relationship being an appropriate balance between intimacy and autonomy has some meaning for partners. I do believe that some degree of parity in the time available for partners to be themselves is a crucial factor in a relationship. If support and choice are available to AS and NT partners (or partners in any relationship for that matter) then these two elements, particularly when working in tandem, have the capacity to bring with them rich rewards for the relationship.

Chapter 8

Conclusion – Where Are We Now?

Good actions give strength to ourselves and inspire good actions in others.

Plato

When I first thought about creating a model for counselling AS–NT couples, I needed to know if anything was already in place. If there was then it would render my goal as well intended, but unnecessary. I was already aware of Christopher Slater-Walker's views from his and his wife Gisela's book *An Asperger Marriage* that such a counselling model didn't exist, but there may well have been some work already underway to correct this situation.

I thought it would be appropriate to contact certain people 'in the know' to check out my query and so I started with Autism West Midlands. When I explained that I was researching couple counselling for AS–NT couples, my enquiry was greeted with much interest, but I was told, 'You are probably venturing into uncharted territory.' A subsequent call to the National Autistic Society brought the response 'There has been very little research done in this area' and that 'there is a definite gap in the market for this form of counselling'. So far it seemed that Christopher Slater-Walker's views could be upheld.

Upon recommendation, I wrote to Professor Digby Tantam at Sheffield University, to enquire if he was aware of any articles or papers that would suggest a counselling model such as I proposed was either in place or being considered. Professor Tantam is a world-renowned author and lecturer on autistic matters and he kindly responded to me saying that he wasn't aware of any such literature. With three such responses, from Autism West Midlands, the National Autistic Society and Professor Tantam, I felt it was safe to assume that no such counselling model existed and that it was appropriate and important for me to proceed.

The research I undertook and the formulation of my counselling model are discussed in Chapter 1, and although the consecutive chapters of this book describe the stages of the model, it is not actually presented anywhere in its complete form. I intend to remedy that now.

The Thompson model for counselling couples where Asperger Syndrome is a presenting problem in the relationship

Stage 1 – Understanding Asperger Syndrome
The Counsellor has to have a good knowledge and understanding of AS issues.

Stage 2 – Individual counselling
Initial counselling should be separate for both partners so their own needs can be understood before co-counselling commences, and should remain an option later on in the process.

Stage 3 – Co-counselling begins
Co-counselling commences – reading or video materials should be considered to help develop a conjoint understanding of AS issues, emotions and personalities.

Stage 4 – Acknowledging different perspectives
Communication – issues of clarification, interpretation, translation and general awareness should be developed between the partners.

Stage 5 – Visual aids for understanding: What the counsellor does
Genograms, flip charts, drawings and other written materials can be used to aid understanding for and between the partners.

Stage 6 – Developing strategies: What the Clients do
Lists, tasks, strategies and other written memorandums can be used to improve communication, aid memory and develop non-intrusive routines.

Stage 7 – Ongoing support and personal space
A balance of intimacy and autonomy should be sought for both AS and NT partners via support groups and their own personal space.

I have used this model with a high degree of success since it's conception in 2002. That's not to say that I have had success with every AS–NT couple that I have counselled, of course not, because there have been some cases where there appears to have been relatively little benefit to my clients. That said, I don't consider this to be an indictment of the model, perhaps it was the case that any change for the partners, particularly the AS one, was just too much for them to handle. I have now had five years of trialling the model in order to test its effectiveness and I remain confident about it. Accordingly, I continue to be indebted to the AS people and their partners who helped me with my initial research and therefore the formulation of the model.

When I first started using the model I thought I knew a lot about AS, but on reflection I didn't really know very much about it at all. Five years down the line I have learned so much more. There's a truism in the world of counselling and therapy and it is that we very often receive as much, if not more from our clients than we give to them. Certainly it is the case for me that I have received enormous insight into the Asperger world from so many people in it. One might think that because of my own AS traits I would already have known all about that world, but why should I? Does an NT person know all there is to know about their world? I think not. I was only previously aware of my own personal perspective.

I would remind readers that I have never met an AS–NT couple who are not unique or met two AS people who are the same. In apparent contradiction to this, 'The apple doesn't fall far from the tree' is a saying often used in genealogical terms to suggest that a son will bear many of the personality traits of the father. However, this should not be applied to AS in the same way just because the genetic code that pre-determines our characteristics may apply from a physical perspective, because if the brain is 'wired up' differently, then even though fathers and sons who have both been diagnosed with AS may bear strikingly similar physical characteristics, the potential for difference between them behaviourally is such that an independent observer wouldn't believe they shared the same condition.

Although we define AS by way of poor socialisation skills, poor communication skills and a lack of imaginative thinking, the scope for difference between such people within these deficits is immense. If we add into this 'cocktail' the considerable number of traits that are aligned to AS, all of which are a spectrum within themselves, we can see that the 'apple' can and does fall far from the 'tree' insofar as the differences between any two AS people are concerned. Such is the variation in AS that even an NT person who comes to know AS in a particular individual may not recognise it in someone less well known to them.

AS with its triad of impairments and all of its various traits, some possessed by some AS people, others not; the variety of special interests that some AS people exhibit; the honesty, the sadness, the humour and the confusion; the emotions that are felt, but are very often difficult to express have all been opened up to me over the course of the last five years by the many AS–NT clients that I've had, and I will be eternally grateful to them. In many ways they have enabled me to make more sense of my own life.

They know who they are and I can only hope that I have given back to them in equal measure.

So we can now accept that AS is not always an easily recognisable ailment that is externally obvious such as a man with a plaster cast on his leg or arm, indicating that he probably has a fractured bone. Neither is the remedy as straightforward in that broken bones can be mended, sometimes with the assistance of a variety of pins, metal plates, rods and screws, whereas the remedy for AS (where it's possible to achieve one) is through a cognitive-behavioural process that can take a considerable amount of time to learn. Furthermore, where broken bones have healed, they are said to be stronger, but there is sometimes a tendency with AS people to learn a new way of doing something and then over the course of time to 'backslide' into a position of unlearning it again.

Where I feel my counselling model benefits AS–NT couples in overcoming the risk of backsliding is that it is a progressive model, designed to be built layer upon layer as awareness and knowledge grow within the individuals and the relationship. In this progressive manner the counselling model doesn't overwhelm people (particularly the AS partner), and it doesn't feel to them as if things are advancing too prematurely. Sometimes though, the most that an AS person can achieve in terms of gaining awareness and knowledge of the issues involved is the shock discovery that other people don't see the world as they do! But even this is still progress.

It needs to be said at this juncture that timing can be an issue of contention between AS and NT partners in counselling, as the NT partner may understandably want things to progress as quickly as possible to Stage Six of the model (doing the tasks, strategies etc.), whereas the AS partner is much more likely to want to embrace the changes to his life more slowly and methodically, with as much advance notice as possible of what the changes might be and how they will impact upon him.

Moving too quickly through the stages can feel threatening to the AS partner and it is crucial that he remains on board with this form of therapy or he may decide to 'abandon ship' and have nothing more to do with it. Moving too slowly can have the effect of the already frustrated NT partner not being able to withstand any more pressure, and so she may become even further discouraged and conclude counselling also. This is a difficult call for the counsellor as the frustrated needs of the NT partner have to be constantly balanced with the AS partner's cautious concerns, but where this balance can be achieved and the model applied in the way I suggest, then progress can be made and a benefit to the relationship has been the usual outcome of the therapy I have experienced with my clients.

Whilst I am clearly advocating that the model be applied systematically, stage by stage for couple counselling, I do not believe this renders the immediate use of the strategies in Stage Six as inappropriate where children or young persons are concerned. Let me explain. Couple counselling relies on not just a change in the way things are done, but on an understanding that there is a different perspective in the relationship, namely that of the other partner. It is also usual for older people (particularly older AS people) to take longer to adapt to change. The old adage 'You can't teach an old dog new tricks' comes to mind (in point of fact you can teach old dogs new tricks, it's usually the trainers or the training techniques that are inadequate). However, the earlier we can identify AS in a child, the greater the opportunity to implement early interventions and make positive changes in their social and communication skills.

Now I know that children are also in relationships, with parents, with siblings, with friends, but these relationships are different. Children don't have the experiences of older people and are not so set in their ways, but rather they rely on the life-training skills that parents and other primary care givers impart to them. Also the balance of power and control in an adult relationship should be shared and equal between the partners, and the model caters for this by allowing the partners to become aware and gain knowledge simultaneously. In a parent–child relationship the power and control (with all ethical and legal aspects considered) should be in favour of the parent, and so the child comes to trust that the parent knows what is best for them. Because of this, the various strategies of Stage Six of the model (or adapted or similar ones to them) can be selected by the parent for the child to use without the need to undergo the preceding stages of the model.

I have already stated that the number of counsellors and therapists working in the United Kingdom with adult couples affected by AS is limited. In part I feel this is because some are unaware of what AS is, whilst many others, although having some insight into it, don't have the confidence to address it in the therapeutic process. In writing this book I hope that the AS territory has now been charted, that the gap in the market has now been bridged and that my counselling model will provide counsellors and therapists with the confidence to put it into practice, largely because the model and it's strategies are based on the views of clients, but also because it has stood the test of time and continues to work. It is very much a client-centred, uniquely tailored form of therapy that can offer couples affected by AS an opportunity to understand the condition, receive some form of relief from their anxieties and look forward to sharing in a relationship that not only improves, but endures.

Good luck,
Barrie Thompson

References

Articles

Barrow, N. (2004) 'The Truth is I'm Exhausting to Live with.' *Guardian*, Wednesday 26 May 2004.

Bell, P. (2006) 'Who is the Client?' Relate Good Practice Document Library, Wednesday 1 July 2006.

Grove, V. (2002) 'My Darling Stranger'. *The Times*, Saturday 16 February 2002.

Miller, L. (2001) 'Why Won't He Talk to Me'. Life on Saturday.

Slater-Walker, G. (2003) 'At Last You Can Say, "I Love You".' *Woman's Weekly*, Tuesday 16 September 2003.

Books

Gray, C. and White, A. L. (2002) *My Social Stories Book*. London: Jessica Kingsley Publishers.

Holliday Willey, L. (1999) *Pretending To Be Normal: Living with Asperger Syndrome*. London: Jessica Kingsley Publishers.

Holliday Willey, L. (2001) *Asperger Syndrome in the Family: Redefining Normal*. London: Jessica Kingsley Publishers.

Jackson, L. (2002) *Freaks, Geeks and Asperger Syndrome: A User Guide to Adolescence*. London: Jessica Kingsley Publishers.

Sack, O. (1995) *An Anthropologist on Mars*. London: Picador Books.

Scarf, M. (1988) *Intimate Partners: Patterns in Love and Marriage*. New York: Ballantine Books.

Slater-Walker, G and Slater-Wallker C. (2002) *An Asperger Marriage*. London: Jessica Kingsley Publishers.

Welton, J. (2004) *Can I Tell You About Asperger Syndrome: A Guide for Friends and Family*. London: Jessica Kingsley Publishers.

DVDs and Videos

'As Good As It Gets'. (1997) TriStar Pictures.

'Asperger Syndrome: A Different Mind'. (2006) National Autistic Society.

'Mozart and the Whale'. (2005) Big City Pictures.

'Snow Cake'. (2006). Revolution Films.

'Outside In, Living With Asperger Syndrome'. (2002) National Autistic Society.

'Whichever Way You Look At It, It's Still Autism'. (2006) National Autistic Society.

Websites

Autism West Midlands – www.autismwestmidlands.org.uk

National Autistic Society – www.nas.org.uk

The Asperger Society – www.aspergersociety.com

Edinburgh Lothian Asperger Society – www.elas-scot.org.uk

FAAAS – www.faaas.org

Index

Note: the letter 'f' following a page number
    refers to a figure; the letter 'h' refers to a
    handout

5WH principle 97–8, 113–14h

acceptance of AS diagnosis 31–2, 34–5,
    128
    see also non-acceptance of AS diagnosis
acknowledging different perspectives, as
    co-counselling begins 18, 19, 32–3
acknowledging different perspectives (Stage
    4)
    Cassandra phenomenon 54–5
    central coherence theory 50–2, 53f, 58,
        62, 63f, 82h
    differences in traits in AS 45–6, 45f
    elements of communication 43–4
    executive functioning 52, 53f, 61
    humour 46–8, 47f, 48f
    'Mirror Syndrome' 55
    neurological model 47–8, 47f, 48f
    normality versus uniqueness 41–2
    processing time 52–4
    respect for difference 42, 43f
    theory of mind 49–50, 52, 53f, 58, 62,
        63f, 81h
adolescents with AS 15, 21, 126
    see also young people with AS
'adult' ego state 62, 63f, 64, 83h
affection 24, 35, 38, 89, 90, 92
aggressiveness 29
    see also anger; emotional outbursts
agreements, personal space arrangements
    132–3
Alison 128
anger
    expression, strategies developed by clients
        24, 90–1, 91f, 92, 93, 94, 110h
    expression inability, as individual
        counselling 'Issue' 24, 90
    of NP partner 29, 38, 53, 54
'Anger Scratchpad' 90–1, 91f, 92, 94,
    110h
Anne see Case Study 1 – Anne and Bob
Anthropologist on Mars, An (Sack) 38
arguments 29, 106–7, 108, 121–2h
articles, journal 33–9, 139
As Good As It Gets 40
AS partners
    ongoing support for 129
    personal space 130, 131–2, 133
Asperger Identification Cards 126
Asperger Marriage, An (Slater-Walker and
    Slater-Walker) 15, 21, 26, 49, 134
Asperger Society 126
Asperger Syndrome: A Different Mind 39
Asperger Syndrome (AS)
    diagnosis 15, 23, 26, 31–2, 34–5, 38,
        127, 128
    knowledge and understanding 17–21
    organisations 125–7

personal perspective of author 13–14,
    136–7
traits see traits of AS
Asperger Syndrome in the Family (Holliday
    Willey) 73
'At Last You Can Say I Love You'
    (Slater-Walker) 34–5
attentional energy model 58–62, 60–1f,
    79–80h
attitudes 69–71, 70f, 85h
'Attraction,' individual counselling aspect
    23, 24, 25, 26, 27, 28, 29
Autism West Midlands 125–6, 129, 134
autonomy-intimacy balance 130–3, 130f

'baby' role 127, 128
Barbara see Case Study 2 – Barbara and
    Chris
Barrow, N. 36–7
behaviour
    emotional outbursts and Betari Box
        strategy 69–71, 70f, 85h
    inflexible 28
    transactional analysis 64–5, 65f, 83h
Betari Box strategy 69–71, 70f, 85h
Birmingham 129
Bob see Case Study 1 – Anne and Bob
books 18, 21, 139
brain see attentional energy model; central
    coherence theory; executive
    functioning; information processing
    time; theory of mind

calming effects see Betari Box strategy;
    comfort kits; Traffic Light Cards
    strategy
Can I Tell You about Asperger Syndrome
    (Welton) 21
Carol see Case Study 3 – Carol and Doug
Case Study 1 – Anne and Bob
    individual counselling (Stage 2) 23–5,
        89–90, 94–5
    strategies see strategies developed in Case
        Study 1 – Anne and Bob
Case Study 2 – Barbara and Chris
    individual counselling (Stage 2) 25–6, 97
    strategies see strategies developed in Case
        Study 2 – Barbara and Chris
Case Study 3 – Carol and Doug
    individual counselling (Stage 2) 26–8,
        104
    strategies see strategies developed in Case
        Study 3 – Carol and Doug
Case Study 4 – Diane and Eric
    individual counselling (Stage 2) 28–9
    strategies see strategies developed in Case
        Study 4 – Diane and Eric
Cassandra phenomenon 54–5
central coherence theory 50–2, 53f, 58, 62,
    63f, 82h
chameleon effect 32, 50, 54–5
changing the subject 53, 54
'child' ego state 62, 63f, 64–5, 65f, 83h

children, and genograms 65, 66f, 67–8,
    84h
children with AS 15, 21, 39, 125, 126,
    138
Chris see Case Study 2 – Barbara and Chris
clarification 43, 44
client-based NT support groups 123–4
client–counsellor relationship 30
clients
    individual versus relationship as client
        22–3, 42
    strategies developed by see developing
        strategies: what the clients do
        (Stage 6)
    strategies developed for see visual aids for
        understanding: what the counsellor
        does (Stage 5)
co-counselling begins (Stage 3)
    acceptance of Asperger Syndrome (AS) by
        NP partner 31–2, 34–5
    articles for discussion 33–9
    films for discussion 39–40
    importance of acknowledging different
        perspectives 32–3
cognitive processes see attentional energy
    model; central coherence theory;
    executive functioning; information
    processing time; theory of mind
colleagues, and Cassandra phenomenon
    54–5
colours 92, 93f, 94, 107, 111h
comfort cards 73–4, 74f, 75, 87h
comfort kits 73–5, 74f, 87h
communication
    Daily and Weekly Timetables strategies
        98–9, 99f, 100, 115–16h
    elements 43–4
    individual counselling 'Want' 25, 26, 27,
        29
    notes, use of 90, 92, 101, 102f, 104,
        105
    Relationship jigsaw strategy 95–7, 95f,
        96f, 112h
    transactional analysis 62–5, 63f, 65f,
        83h
    see also arguments; communication
        difficulties; e-mail; emotional
        outbursts; intimacy; iPods;
        messages; mobile phones;
        telephone conversations; telephone
        counselling; white-board strategy
communication difficulties
    articles about Asperger couples 34, 35,
        37
    'distant' moments and counting
        compulsion 46–7
    'distant' moments and humour 47–8
    face-to-face communication 107
    individual counselling 'Issue' 24, 25, 26,
        27, 90, 94, 100
    'Triad of Impairment' of Asperger
        Syndrome (AS) 17, 136
conflict prevention and resolution 29,
    106–7, 108, 120–1h

Conflict Prevention Plan 106, 107, 120h
Constructive Discussion 106–7, 121h
counselling for Asperger couples,
    Thompson model *see* Thompson
    model for counselling Asperger
    couples
counsellor, visual aids for understanding *see*
    visual aids for understanding: what
    the counsellor does (Stage 5)
counsellor–client relationship 30
counsellors, as facilitators in client-based
    NT support groups 124
counting compulsion 46–7
couple versus individual as client 22–3, 42
Coventry 124, 129
Coventry Social Services 129
Criminal Justice Forum 126
'critical parent' ego state 63f, 64–5, 65f,
    69, 71, 83h
criticism 28, 124, 125, 128

Daily Timetable strategy 98, 99f, 100,
    115h, 132
developing strategies: what the clients do
    (Stage 6) 89, 107–8, 137–8
    see also strategies developed in Case Study
        1 – Anne and Bob; strategies
        developed in Case Study 2 –
        Barbara and Chris; strategies
        developed in Case Study 3 – Carol
        and Doug; strategies developed in
        Case Study 4 – Diane and Eric
diagnosis of Asperger Syndrome (AS) 15,
    23, 26, 31–2, 34–5, 38, 127, 128
    see also Cassandra phenomenon
Diane *see* Case Study 4 – Diane and Eric
'distant' moments 46–8, 47f, 48f, 53–4
Doug *see* Case Study 3 – Carol and Doug
DVDs 39–40, 139

e-mail 108, 124
Edinburgh Lothian Asperger Society (ELAS)
    126
educational support 125, 126
ego states, in transactional analysis 62–5,
    63f, 65f, 69, 71, 83h
electronic communication 108, 124
emotion
    communicating, as individual counselling
        'Issue' 26
    transactional analysis 63f, 64–5, 65f
    versus logic 106, 107
    see also affection; anger; arguments;
        comfort kits; emotional outbursts;
        emotional 'risk'; emotional security;
        emotional suffocation; frustration;
        hugs; intimacy; kisses; moods;
        ongoing support and personal
        space (Stage 7)
emotional outbursts
    Betari Box strategy 69–71, 70f, 85h
    Traffic Light Cards strategy 71–3, 72f,
        86h
emotional 'risk' 94–5
emotional security 130
emotional suffocation 130, 131
employment support 125, 126
energy, attentional model 58–62, 60–1f,
    79–80h
Eric *see* Case Study 4 – Diane and Eric
event planning difficulties 98, 100, 114h
Event Planning strategy 98, 100, 114h
exclusion 24, 90
    see also inclusion; isolation
executive functioning 52, 53f, 61

face-to-face communication difficulties 107

facilitation, in client-based NT support
    groups 124
'facilitative' role, in transactional analysis
    63f, 64
families
    Cassandra phenomenon 54–5
    genograms 65–9, 66f, 84h
    ongoing support for 125, 126–7, 128
    ongoing support from 123, 127–8
Families of Adults Affected by Asperger
    Syndrome (FAAAS) 54, 55, 126–7
father role 27, 29, 128
films 39–40, 139
First Order theory of mind 49–50
forgetfulness 100–1, 101f, 105
Freaks, Geeks and Asperger Syndrome (Jackson)
    21
friends 54–5, 123, 127–8
frustration
    expression, as individual counselling
        'Issue' 90
    expression, strategies: developed by
        clients 24, 90, 92, 93
    of NP partner 29, 38, 53, 54

genograms 65–9, 66f, 84h
geographically located NT support 124–5
Grandin, Temple 38
Gray, C. 21, 89
Grove, V. 37–8

handouts 76–87, 109–21
Holliday Willey, L. 41–2, 73
hugs 24, 35, 89, 90, 92
humour 46–8, 47f, 48f, 136
husband role 27, 28, 128

Ian 127–8
imaginative thinking difficulties 17, 136
inclusion 29, 92, 93f, 94, 111h
    see also exclusion; isolation
individual counselling (Stage 2)
    Case study 1 – Anne and Bob 23–5,
        94–5
    Case study 2 – Barbara and Chris 25–6
    Case study 3 – Carol and Doug 26–8,
        104
    Case study 4 – Diane and Eric 28–9
    counsellor–client relationship 30
    importance 22–3, 29–30
individual versus relationship as client
    22–3, 42
inflexible behaviour 28
information 18–20, 21, 128
    see also articles, journal; communication;
        films; information overload;
        knowledge; messages; notes;
        reminders; timetable strategies;
        websites
information overload 17, 51–2, 57–8, 58f
information processing time 52–4, 106
intelligence 24, 25, 26
intensity of AS relationship 130–1
interpretation 43, 44
interviews, research 19–20, 131
intimacy
    autonomy balance 130–3, 130f
    individual counselling 'Issue' 24, 27, 89,
        100
    individual counselling 'Want' 27
    strategies developed by clients 90, 92,
        104, 105, 119h
Intimacy Task 104, 105, 119h
Intimate Partners (Scarf) 104
iPods 74–5, 87h
isolation 37, 55, 122–3, 128
    see also exclusion; inclusion

'Issues'
    co-counselling 89–90, 94–5, 97, 100,
        105–6
    individual counselling 23, 24, 25, 26,
        27–9
    prioritisation exercises 57–8, 57f, 59f,
        77h, 78h

Jackson, L. 21
journal articles 33–9, 139

kisses 24, 89, 90, 92
knowledge 17–21, 128
    see also communication; information;
        understanding Asperger Syndrome
        (Stage 1)

learned social skills 34, 37
    see also chameleon effect
literalness 17
logic versus emotion 106, 107
Lucy 127–8

manifestos of commitment 108
men with AS, ratio to women 31
mental exhaustion 58–62, 60–1f, 79–80h
messages
    comfort cards 73–4, 74f, 75, 87h
    electronic 108
    reminders 101, 101f, 105
    teddy bear visual message 108
Miller, L. 35
mind, theory of 49–50, 53f, 58, 62, 63f,
    81h
'Mirror Syndrome' 55
mobile phones 75, 87h, 105, 108
moods 92, 93f, 94, 107, 111h
motor skill deficits 17
Mozart and the Whale 40
music, in comfort kits 75, 87h
'My Darling Stranger' (Grove) 37–8
My Social Stories Book (Gray and White) 21,
    89

National Autistic Society 34, 35, 39, 51,
    125, 134
'naughty child' ego state 63f, 64–5, 65f,
    83h
negative behaviour cycles 64–5, 65f,
    69–71, 70f, 85h
negative experiences 124, 125, 127–8
    see also 'Issues'
neurological model of AS 47–8, 47f, 48f
non-acceptance of AS diagnosis 31–2,
    127–8
    see also acceptance of AS diagnosis
normality versus uniqueness 41–2, 43f
notes 90, 92, 101, 102f, 104, 105, 117h
    see also messages; reminders
NP people, 'world of gist' 51, 57
NT partners
    acceptance of Asperger Syndrome (AS)
        diagnosis 31–2, 34–5
    Cassandra phenomenon 54–5
    ongoing support 122–5
    personal space 130, 131–2, 133

obsessions *see* special interests
obsessive compulsive disorder (OCD) 13,
    36–7, 40, 46–7
ongoing support and personal space (Stage
    7)
ongoing support
    AS partner 129
    Asperger couple 125–8
    NT partner 122–5
    personal space 130–3

orderliness 17, 36, 38, 46
organisations 125–7
Outside In: Living with Asperger Syndrome 39

parents
    counselling for Asperger couples 15
    developing strategies: what the client
        does (Stage 6) 138
    ego state 62, 63f, 64–5, 65f, 69, 71, 83h
    genograms 65, 67–8, 66f, 69, 84h
    information about children with AS 21
    see also father role
personal perspective of author 13–14,
    136–7
perspectives *see* acknowledging different
        perspectives, as co-counselling
        begins; acknowledging different
        perspectives (Stage 4); personal
        perspective of author
phones *see* mobile phones; telephone
        conversations; telephone counselling;
        text messages
photographs, in comfort kits 73–4, 75, 87h
'prescriptive' role, in transactional analysis
    62, 63f, 64–5, 69, 71, 83h
Pretending to be Normal (Holliday Willey)
    41–2
prioritisation of issues exercises 57–8, 57f,
    59f, 77h, 78h
processing time 52–4, 106
proprioception 50–1
psychological processes *see* attentional
        energy model; central coherence
        theory; executive functioning;
        information processing time; theory
        of mind; transactional analysis

Question Cards strategy 103f, 104, 105,
    118h
quietness 24, 25, 26

reading 128
    see also articles, journal; books
'receptive' role, in transactional analysis
    63f, 64
Relate 9, 22–3, 42
Relationship Jigsaw strategy 95–7, 95f,
    96f, 112h
relationship see-saw 130–3, 130f
relationships
    genograms 65–9, 66f, 84h
    Relationship Jigsaw strategy 95–7, 95f,
        96f, 112h
    transactional analysis 62–5, 63f, 65f,
        83h
    understanding of, as individual
        counselling 'Issue' 94–5
    versus individuals as client 22–3, 42
reminders 101, 101f, 105
    see also notes
repeating questions, and information
        processing time 53, 54
research methods 9–10, 18–20
respect for different perspective 42, 43f
responsibility issues 27, 28, 100–1, 101f,
    105, 131
rewards 132–3
Rick 128
'risk,' emotional 94–5
rituals 35, 46–7
    see also obsessive compulsive disorder
        (OCD); routines; rules; special
        interests
roles
    genograms 65, 66f, 67, 68, 84h
    transactional analysis 62–5, 63f, 65f, 69,
        71, 83h

see also 'baby' role; father role; husband
        role
routines 24, 28–9, 36, 38
    see also obsessive compulsive disorder
        (OCD); orderliness; rituals; rules
rules 24, 65, 66f, 67, 84h
    see also obsessive compulsive disorder
        (OCD); orderliness; rituals; routines

Sack, O. (*An Anthropologist on Mars*) 38
Scarf, M. 104
Scotland 126
Second Order theory of mind 49–50
self-help groups 123–5, 128
sensory information 17, 50–2, 53f, 58
shared feelings
    individual counselling 'Want' 24
    strategies developed by clients 90, 92,
        93f, 94, 111h
    'What Colour Are You Feeling?' 92, 93f,
        94, 111h
shared interests 24, 29, 34, 37–8
shared thoughts 24
shared time together 130, 131, 132–3
    see also intimacy
siblings, in genograms 65, 66f, 67–8, 84h
Slater-Walker, C. 15, 21, 26, 34–5, 37–8,
    49, 134
Slater-Walker, G. 15, 21, 26, 34–5, 37–8,
    49, 134
Snow Cake 40
social awkwardness 34, 35, 37, 38, 106
social groups 123, 129
social skills, learned 34, 37
    see also chameleon effect
social stories 89
socialisation difficulties 17, 136
spatial skill deficit 17
special interests 13, 17, 35, 36–7, 131–2,
    133, 136
spiritual closeness 130
stability 29
    see also arguments; conflict prevention and
        resolution
strategies *see* developing strategies: what the
        clients do (Stage 6); strategies
        developed in Case Study 1 – Anne
        and Bob; strategies developed in
        Case Study 2 – Barbara and Chris;
        strategies developed in Case Study 3
        – Carol and Doug; strategies
        developed in Case Study 4 – Diane
        and Eric; visual aids for
        understanding: what the counsellor
        does (Stage 5)
strategies developed in Case Study 1 –
        Anne and Bob
    Issues and Wants 89–90, 94–5
    review of strategies 92, 94–5
    Strategy 1: intimacy problem and use of
        notes 90, 92
    Strategy 2: expressing anger and 'Anger
        Scratchpad' 90–1, 91f, 92, 93,
        110h
    Strategy 3: inclusion and 'What Colour
        Are You Feeling?' 92, 93f, 94,
        111h
    Strategy 4: Relationship Jigsaw 95–7,
        95f, 96f, 112h
strategies developed in Case Study 2 –
        Barbara and Chris
    Issues and Wants 97
    review of strategies 100
    Strategy 1: Task Planning and 5WH
        principle 97, 100, 113h
    Strategy 2: Event Planning and 5WH
        principle 98, 100, 114h
    Strategy 3: Daily Timetable strategy 98,
        99f, 100, 115h

Strategy 4: Weekly Timetable strategy
        98–9, 100, 116h
strategies developed in Case Study 3 –
        Carol and Doug
    Issues and Wants 100
    review of strategies 105
    Strategy 1: responsibility issues and
        white-board 100–1, 101f, 105
    Strategy 2: communication problems and
        use of notes 101, 102f, 104, 105,
        117h
    Strategy 3: communication problems and
        Question Cards 103f, 104, 105,
        118h
    Strategy 4: Intimacy Task 104, 105,
        119h
strategies developed in Case Study 4 –
        Diane and Eric
    Issues and Wants 105–6
    Strategy 1: Conflict Prevention Plan 106,
        107, 120h
    Strategy 2: Constructive Discussion
        106–7, 121h
stress reduction *see* Betari Box strategy;
        comfort kits; Traffic Light Cards
        strategy
suffocation, emotional 130, 131
support, ongoing *see* ongoing support and
        personal space (Stage 7)

Tantam, Digby 9, 134
task planning difficulties 97, 100
Task Planning strategy 97, 100, 113h
teddy bear visual message 108
telephone conversations 103f, 104, 105,
    107–8, 118h
telephone counselling 124
text messages 108
theory of mind 49–50, 52, 53f, 58, 62,
    63f, 81h
Thompson model for counselling Asperger
        couples
    children and young people, use of 138
    demand for 9, 10
    development 9–10, 14, 18–21, 134–5
    importance 10–11, 15, 138
    presentation of 135
        see also acknowledging different
            perspectives (Stage 4);
            co-counselling begins (Stage 3);
            developing strategies: what the
            clients do (Stage 6); ongoing
            support and personal space
            (Stage 7); understanding
            Asperger Syndrome (Stage 1);
            visual aids for understanding:
            what the counsellor does (Stage
            5); individual counselling (Stage
            2)
    progressiveness 137
    research methods 9–10, 18–20
    successfulness 135–6, 138
    timing of stages 136–7
timetable strategies 98–100, 99f, 115–16h,
    132
timing of stages of Thompson model for
        counselling Asperger couples 136–7
Traffic Light Cards strategy 71–3, 72f, 86h
traits of AS 17–18, 45–6, 45f, 136–7
    see also chameleon effect; communication
            difficulties; 'distant' moments;
            humour; information overload;
            learned social skills; logic versus
            emotion; obsessive compulsive
            disorder (OCD); quietness; rituals;
            routines; sensory information;
            social awkwardness; special
            interests; 'world of infinite detail'

transactional analysis 62–5, 63f, 65f, 69,
        71, 83h
translation 43–4
'Triad of Impairment' of Asperger
        Syndrome (AS) 17, 136
'Truth Is I'm Exhausting to Live With, The'
        (Barrow) 36–7

understanding Asperger Syndrome (Stage 1)
        17–21
    see also visual aids for understanding: what
        the counsellor does (Stage 5)
uniqueness 10, 41–2, 43f, 88–9, 136
United States 126–7
urn metaphor of attentional energy model
        58–62, 60–1f, 79–80h

vestibular sense 50
videos 39–40, 139
visual aids for understanding: what the
        counsellor does (Stage 5)
    comfort kits 73–5, 74f, 87h
    emotional outbursts and Betari Box
        strategy 69–71, 70f, 85h
    emotional outbursts and Traffic Light
        Cards strategy 71–3, 72f, 86h
    genograms 65–9, 66f, 84h
    mental exhaustion and attentional energy
        model 58–62, 60–1f, 79–80h
    prioritisation of issues exercises 57–8,
        57f, 59f, 77h, 78h
    transactional analysis 62–5, 63f, 65f,
        83h
visual messages 108
'volcanic' metaphor of emotional outbursts
        69–71, 70f, 85h
vulnerability, and transactional analysis
        64–5, 83h

Walker, C. Slater- *see* Slater-Walker, C.
Walker, G. Slater- *see* Slater-Walker, G.
'Wants'
    co-counselling 90, 97, 100, 106
    individual counselling 23, 24, 25, 26,
        27, 28, 29
websites 125–7, 140
Weekly Timetable strategy 98–9, 100,
        116h, 132
Welton, J. 21
West Midlands 125–6, 129
    see also Autism West Midlands
'What Colour Are You Feeling?' strategy
        92, 93f, 94, 107, 111h
Whichever Way You Look at It, It's Still Autism
        39
White, A. L. 21, 89
white-board strategy 100–1, 101f, 105
'Why Won't He Talk To Me?' (Miller) 35
women with AS, ratio to men 31
Worcester 129
'world of gist' 51, 57
'world of infinite detail' 51–2, 57–8, 59f
'Write Notes' 101, 102f, 104, 105, 117h
written agreements, personal space
        arrangements 132–3

young people with AS 21, 138
    see also adolescents with AS; children with
        AS

CPI Antony Rowe
Eastbourne, UK
October 23, 2019